Match of My Life

LEEDS RHINOS

KNOW THE SCORE BOOKS SPORTS PUBLICATIONS

CULT HEROES	Author	ISBN
CARLISLE UNITED	Paul Harrison	978-1-905449-09-7
CELTIC	David Potter	978-1-905449-08-8
CHELSEA	Leo Moynihan	1-905449-00-3
MANCHESTER CITY	David Clayton	978-1-905449-05-7
NEWCASTLE	Dylan Younger	1-905449-03-8
NOTTINGHAM FOREST	David McVay	978-1-905449-06-4
RANGERS	Paul Smith	978-1-905449-07-1
SOUTHAMPTON	Jeremy Wilson	1-905449-01-1
WEST BROM	Simon Wright	1-905449-02-X

MATCH OF MY LIFE	Editor	ISBN
DERBY COUNTY	Nick Johnson	978-1-905449-68-2
ENGLAND WORLD CUP	Massarella & Moynihan	1-905449-52-6
EUROPEAN CUP FINALS	Ben Lyttleton	1-905449-57-7
FA CUP FINALS 1953-1969	David Saffer	978-1-905449-53-8
FULHAM	Michael Heatley	1-905449-51-8
LEEDS	David Saffer	1-905449-54-2
LIVERPOOL	Leo Moynihan	1-905449-50-X
MANCHESTER UNITED	Ivan Ponting	978-1-905449-59-0
SHEFFIELD UNITED	Nick Johnson	1-905449-62-3
STOKE CITY	Simon Lowe	978-1-905449-55-2
SUNDERLAND	Rob Mason	1-905449-60-7
SPURS	Allen & Massarella	978-1-905449-58-3
WOLVES	Simon Lowe	1-905449-56-9

GENERAL FOOTBALL	Author	ISBN
2006 WORLD CUP DIARY	Harry Harris	1-905449-90-9
BEHIND THE BACK PAGE	Christopher Davies	978-1-84818-506-7
BOOK OF FOOTBALL OBITUARIES	Ivan Ponting	978-1-905449-82-2
BURKSEY	Peter Morfoot	1-905449-49-6
HOLD THE BACK PAGE	Harry Harris	1-905449-91-7
MY PREMIERSHIP DIARY	Marcus Hahnemann	978-1-905449-33-0
OUTCASTS	Steve Menary	978-1-905449-31-6
The Lands That FIFA Forgot		
PARISH TO PLANET	Eric Midwinter	978-1-905449-30-9
A History of Football		

TACKLES LIKE A FERRET (England Cover)	Paul Parker	1-905449-47-X
TACKLES LIKE A FERRET (Manchester United Cover)	Paul Parker	1-905449-46-1
THE DOOG	Harrison & Gordos	978-1-84818-502-9
THE RVALS GAME	Douglas Beattie	978-1-905449-79-8

RUGBY LEAGUE	Author	ISBN
MOML LEEDS RHINOS	Caplan & Saffer	978-1-905449-69-9
MOML WIGAN WARRIORS	David Kuzio	978-1-905449-66-8

CRICKET	Author	ISBN
ASHES TO DUST	Graham Cookson	978-1-905449-19-4
CRASH! BANG! WALLOP!	Martyn Hindley	978-1-905449-88-0
GROVEL!	David Tossell	978-1-905449-43-9
MOML: THE ASHES	Pilger & Wightman	1-905449-63-1
MY TURN TO SPIN	Shaun Udal	978-1-905449-42-2
WASTED?	Paul Smith	978-1-905449-45-3

FORTHCOMING PUBLICATIONS IN 2008

MATCH OF MY LIFE	Editor	ISBN
BRIGHTON	Paul Camillin	978-1-84818-000-0
IPSWICH TOWN	Mel Henderson	978-1-84818-001-7

GENERAL FOOTBALL	Author	ISBN
FORGIVE US OUR PRESS PASSES	Football Writers' Association	978-1-84818-507-4
JUST ONE OF SEVEN	Denis Smith	978-1-84818-504-3
MAN & BABE	Wilf McGuinness	978-1-84818-503-6
MANCHESTER UNITED: PLAYER BY PLAYER	Ivan Ponting	978-1-84818-500-1
PALLY	Gary Pallister	978-1-84818-500-5
PLEASE MAY I HAVE MY FOOTBALL BACK?	Eric Alexander	978-1-84818-508-1
TOTTENHAM HOTSPUR: PLAYER BY PLAYER	Ivan Ponting	978-1-84818-501-8

Match of My Life

LEEDS RHINOS

Editors: Phil Caplan & David Saffer

www.knowthescorebooks.com

First published in the United Kingdom
by Know The Score Books Limited, 2008

Know The Score Books Limited
118 Alcester Road
Studley
Warwickshire
B80 7NT
01527 454482
info@knowthescorebooks.com
www.knowthescorebooks.com

A CIP catalogue record is available for this book from the British Library
ISBN: 978-1-905449-69-9

Mixed Sources
Product group from well-managed
forests and other controlled sources
www.fsc.org Cert no. TT-COC-2082
FSC © 1996 Forest Stewardship Council

Jacket design by Lisa David

Printed and bound in Great Britain
By Cromwell Press, Trowbridge, Wiltshire

Front cover:

Top: Winger Leroy Rivett (left) parades the Challenge Cup with skipper Iestyn Harris after the last final at the old Wembley Stadium in 1999. The young winger's feat of scoring four tries set a new landmark in a decider and won him the Lance Todd Trophy.

Middle: Danny McGuire in typical poacher's pose. The ultimate local hero has become a modern day favourite for club and country with a penchant for scoring spectacular tries.

Bottom: Captain Fantastic: current skipper and testimonial recipient Kevin Sinfield is the paragon of the modern professional. In 2007 he became the first player in the club's history to play and score in every match in a
season, culminating in Grand Final glory.

Rear cover:

Top left: Danny McGuire (right) holds up the Carnegie World Club Challenge trophy together with skipper Kevin Sinfield at Elland Road in 2005, the highlight of victory over Australian champions Canterbury Bulldogs being his scintillating try from halfway.

Top right: Leeds' greatest ever servant and one of their classiest performers, Kirkstall-born playmaker John Holmes graced the blue and amber shirt for 21 glorious seasons.

Bottom: The jubilant Rhinos squad celebrate their first title success for 32 years as they lift the Super League trophy at Old Trafford in 2004, in front of a capacity crowd against local rivals Bradford Bulls.

Editor's Acknowledgements

The most important and heartfelt thanks must go to the players catalogued here, who gave so generously and selflessly of their time. They are an enormous credit to the sport they grace.

Similarly, Brian McClennan's ready agreement to write the foreword, while at the same time wondering as to his worthiness for the job, speaks volumes for someone who has made a massive impact in his short time at the Rhinos.

The pictures of the contemporary players are courtesy of the indispensable rlphotos.com and their factotum Dave Williams. The other associated images are taken from the editors' private collection and if any breach of copyright has occurred, it is entirely unintentional.

A debt of gratitude goes to proof readers Ros Caplan and Jonathan Doidge.

Thanks go to Simon Lowe and his staff at Know the Score for their help, assistance and understanding along the way.

Phil Caplan & David Saffer
June 2008

TO JEFF STEVENSON, THE FIRST LOINER
TO WIN AN INDIVIDUAL ACCOLADE IN A DECIDER,
WHOSE UNTIMELY PASSING ON THE EVE OF THE
2007 GRAND FINAL ROBBED US ALL OF
YOUR CONTRIBUTION.

THE PLAYERS

1. **JOHN HOLMES**
   FULL BACK

2. **LEROY RIVETT**
   WING

3. **LEWIS JONES**
   CENTRE

4. **DEREK HALLAS**
   CENTRE

5. **JOHN ATKINSON**
   WING

6. **DANNY MCGUIRE**
   STAND OFF

7. **ROB BURROW**
   SCRUM HALF

8. **ROY DICKINSON**
   PROP

9. **TONY CROSBY**
   HOOKER

10. **STEVE PITCHFORD**
    PROP

11. **BILL RAMSEY**
    SECOND ROW

12. **PAUL MEDLEY**
    SECOND ROW

13. **KEVIN SINFIELD**
    LOOSE FORWARD

Contents

INTRODUCTION   II
Phil Caplan

FOREWORD   IV
Brian McClennan

LEWIS JONES   2
v Barrow
Challenge Cup final, May 1957

DEREK HALLAS   16
v Warrington
Championship final, May 1961

TONY CROSBY   30
v Wakefield Trinity
Challenge Cup final, May 1968

BILL RAMSEY   44
v Castleford
Championship final, May 1969

ROY DICKINSON   56
v St Helens
Premiership Trophy final, May 1975

STEVE PITCHFORD   68
v Widnes
Challenge Cup final, May 1977

JOHN ATKINSON 78
v St Helens
Challenge Cup final, May 1978

JOHN HOLMES 92
v Widnes
John Player Special Trophy final, January 1984

PAUL MEDLEY 104
v Hull Kingston Rovers
Challenge Cup semi-final, March 1986

LEROY RIVETT 116
v London Broncos
Challenge Cup final, May 1999

KEVIN SINFIELD 130
v Bradford Bulls
Super League Grand final, October 2004

DANNY McGUIRE 144
v Canterbury Bulldogs
World Club Challenge, February 2005

ROB BURROW 156
v St Helens
Super League Grand final, October 2007

Introduction

"He was a genius – that is to say, a man who does superlatively and without obvious effort something that most people cannot do by the uttermost exertion of their abilities."

Robertson Davies, 'Fifth Business'

If you don't play, and therefore can't fully understand the dynamics of the game, the next best option is to wallow in the company of the geniuses who have. To be able to do that is also an absolute honour.

The foundation of Rugby League is the honesty, integrity and self-effacing nature of the gladiators; their spirit of sportsmanship and mutual respect – despite the intense ferocity of combat – a lesson to virtually all other sports, many of whom offer far greater riches for much lesser deeds and sacrifices.

It soon became obvious, undertaking this hugely privileged project, that the protagonists also massively undervalue their ability to inspire and the absolute joy and uplift they bring to the multitude.

Those of past generations have produced moments of timeless magic that deserve recording so that the memory and endowment does not dim. Their magnificent contributions should be rightfully recognised, no matter how reticent they may feel about the accolades that followed their exceptional exploits.

Everyone who so freely gave of their time to be included in this collection stressed first and foremost that their achievements were part of a team and wanted to equally fate their collaborators and that is a vital component of these extended interviews.

Those of the current generation are yet to have their accomplishments put into historical context, legacy is retrospective, but there is little doubt that the current Leeds Rhinos era, represented here by Danny McGuire, Rob Burrow and Kevin Sinfield, is rightly being regarded as potentially the best in the club's proud and distinguished history.

The fact that all three men have been an integral part of the summer success and look set to play their entire careers in blue and amber is further testimony to them, loyalty being one of the highest prized and rarest commodities in modern professional sport and all that it entails.

Like every coach through time, one of the biggest dilemmas as a chronicler of a club that has produced some of the greatest names to grace the code, is that of selection.

The hope was to achieve a balance and spread of the memories and to capture not only those who are rightly termed 'generation' players, like Lewis Jones, John Atkinson and John Holmes but others who have, perhaps, rarely had the opportunity to have their exceptional tale told, such as Tony Crosby, Bill Ramsey and Roy Dickinson.

Some names are resonant of a particular golden moment and specific career peak, the likes of Leroy Rivett, Derek Hallas and Steve Pitchford while, there has to be a glorious defeat included to truly capture the essence, drama and emotion of sport, provided here by Paul Medley.

To make the task of who to include deliberately harder, the plan was to come up with a 'team' and, as it turned out, despite being a mythical one, a thirteen which could have conquered the world – to reflect three generations and five decades of legendary players included in these pages.

From Lewis Jones recalling the first modern Wembley win in 1957 to Rob Burrow bringing the story up to date with arguably the greatest performance by a Leeds side in a final fifty years later, the glorious history of one of the Rugby League's most iconic clubs is reflected within these pages by those who helped make and shape it.

Understandably, although the chapters are centred around a specific match, in some respects the exact details of the encounter are secondary to the incidents and circumstances of the time in which they took place and, as a result, wider career reminiscences were deliberately sought from those who so graciously agreed to be involved.

Wonderful memories from special matches by favourite players never fade. Hopefully there are some contained within these pages which will capture the imagination of Leeds and Rugby League fans of all ages.

"He who seldom speaks, and with one calm well-timed word can strike dumb the loquacious, is a genius or a hero."

Johann Kaspar Lavatar

Phil Caplan
June 2008

Foreword

BRIAN McCLENNAN

Even before I took up my post with the Rhinos, I fully appreciated the special, central place that the Leeds club has in the history of the sport I love and grew up in, albeit some 12,000 miles away.

The stellar names who have worn the shirt epitomise so much of the very best rugby league has to offer; flair, invention, commitment and, above all, top quality entertainment and I feel truly honoured to walk in such shadows.

Once I got here, and although I am still in awe as I walk round Headingley Carnegie and all its facilities, I appreciated even more the sense of history that resonates through this unique world venue.

Prior to donning the evocative blue and amber myself, Leeds had special significance for me. In autumn 2004 and then again the following year I was based in the city, near Headingley, with the Kiwis. The occasions could not have been more contrasting or significant, my stay being cut short the first time when I had to fly home in an emergency to tend to my wife Julie.

From pacing up and down the streets in near-despair to the absolute euphoria of picking up the Tri-Nations Trophy almost exactly a year later, at Elland Road, my ties to this great place were established and ingrained.

I am delighted that within this selection of memories, some of the players who I have the privilege to work with are included and rightfully take their place among the pantheon of Leeds greats.

In recent years, especially, the club has worked hard to create an environment that means people don't want to leave and all three of the current squad represented here are the embodiment of that.

Kevin Sinfield is a tremendous leader of our club and someone that everyone holds in the very highest regard. His achievements on the field are only matched by his hard work and commitment to the Leeds cause and the sport as a whole off it. He has already etched his name in Loiners folklore and I am sure he will go on to set many more records in the years ahead; we are all looking forward to helping him do that.

Rob Burrow and Danny McGuire are very popular within the squad, not just as players but as people as well. The team would not be the same without either of them.

I am blessed to work alongside that kind of dedicated professional every day and, as importantly, such quality young men.

Hopefully, we can build on the initial success of winning the World Club Challenge against Melbourne Storm in early 2008 - a match that will surely feature in any follow up compilation to this one for its raw courage, heroism, bravery and sheer will to win in the most trying of conditions.

I'm also fortunate to have met some of the true legends and characters who grace these pages; like Lewis Jones, John Atkinson and Roy Dickinson.

It is so important for present and future generations that their deeds and memories of such glorious occasions written about here – which form the back drop for us all – are captured and enjoyed for posterity.

Enjoy the read.

'Bluey'

Brian McClennan
Head Coach, Leeds Rhinos
June 2008

LEWIS JONES
CENTRE/STAND-OFF 1952–1964

BORN 11 April 1931
SIGNED From Llanelli Rugby Union
LEEDS CAREER 385 appearances, 144 tries, 1,244 goals
HONOURS Championship 1961; Challenge Cup 1957; Yorkshire League Championship 1954/55, 1956/57, 1960/61; Yorkshire Cup 1958; 15 Great Britain caps, 1 Welsh cap, 2 Other Nationalities caps
LEFT To become player/coach at Wentworthville, Australia

Almost 45 years after he hung up his metronomic boots at Headingley, Lewis Jones remains the hero of a generation, his talents still spoken of in reverential terms and viewed by many as the greatest player ever to pull on the famous blue and amber colours. Variously described as a genius and enigma, unique or infuriating, the 'Golden Boy' remains the highest points scorer (2,920) and most prolific goal kicker in the history of the club, while his official seasonal total of 496 in 1956/57 is still the greatest haul the sport has seen. An artist with the ball in hand and world renowned for his trademark hitch kick acceleration, uncanny timing and hanging pass, he was one of the greatest crowd pullers of his time.

Leeds 9 v Barrow 7

Challenge Cup final
Saturday 11 May 1957

Wembley Stadium
Attendance 76,318

Leeds win at Wembley for the first time in 21 years as Lewis Jones caps off a remarkable season by setting up Del Hodgkinson for a crucial try

Teams

Pat Quinn	1	Joe Ball
Delmos Hodgkinson	2	Jimmy Lewthwaite
Keith McLellan	3	Phil Jackson
Lewis Jones	4	Johnny Rea
George Broughton	5	Frank Castle
Jack Lendill	6	Willie Horne
Jeff Stevenson	7	John Harris
Joe Anderson	8	George Woosey
Bernard Prior	9	Maurice Redhead
Bill Hopper	10	Reg Parker
Bernard Poole	11	Jack Grundy
Don Robinson	12	Donald Wilson
Harry Street	13	Bill Healey
Quinn, Hodgkinson, Robinson	Tries	Jackson
	Goals	Horne 2

Referee: Charlie Appleton (Warrington)

THE 1956/57 SEASON WAS an 'annus mirabilis' for Leeds' Welsh maestro Lewis Jones, who averaged an unprecedented ten points a game. Including the Lazenby Cup friendly with Hunslet, he became the first player to post over 500 points in a single season, although that total does not include three matches he played for a British XIII against a French XIII in South Africa which yielded a further 29 goals, five tries and 73 points. A masterful entertainer and match winner, who brought the best out of those around him, he was good enough to play in every back role during his Loiners and Great Britain career – his 385 games for Leeds being broken down into 231 at centre, 117 as stand off, 35 in the full back shirt and once on each wing. In one spell during this glorious campaign he played in ten different positions in successive matches.

The highlight during that 1957 season was the Challenge Cup triumph, especially as it had been 21 years since Leeds had last won at Wembley. The cup run was a glorious one, over 5,000 fans being locked out at Headingley against Wigan in the opening round and a seminal victory coming at fortress Thrum Hall when the Loiners defied a seemingly insurmountable ten point deficit.

Lewis Jones will be remembered in the record books for his momentous kicking feats, his staccato run up and perfect follow through seeing him bang goals over from virtually any angle or distance. He loved nothing better and took even greater pride in setting up and scoring tries. Although, bizarrely, given the feats of the season, his name did not feature on the score sheet at the Empire Stadium, Wembley there was no disputing his genius in setting up Del Hodgkinson for his stunning try, all of which he recalls here.

I HAVE BEEN FORTUNATE to play in a lot of high profile matches throughout my rugby career but my philosophy was always a simple one – to enjoy each and every game whether it was as a schoolboy or in an international. Perhaps because of the number of matches I played in overall, and that desire to make the most of them at the time, I tend not to clearly remember detail. To be honest, I can't really understand why people still want to talk to me about my exploits and recall them with such relish, it was all such a long time ago but if I gave them pleasure and they have fond memories then that is very satisfying.

I'm often asked which was my favourite position; full back, centre or stand off and the answer has always been the same. I always thought that centre was the one that most suited my style of play.

Occasions never really bothered me but one that clearly did was at Wembley in 1957. Despite everything else I'd experienced on the field up until then – playing in the Five Nations for Wales as a teenager, going on tour with the Lions – nothing prepared me for running out at the near-full Empire Stadium at Wembley. Leeds hadn't won the Cup there for a good number of years and to have so many people so desperate for success weighed heavy on us all.

Whenever or wherever I've played, attack and the unorthodox were my watchwords, not tactics or an over focus on technique. Even the greatest defences, in either code, can't cope with the unpredictable. Quite often, when in possession, I had no preconceived idea of what I was going to do so it would be difficult for the opposition to know and counter it. Even when I was coaching, in Australia at Wentworthville and when I returned to Leeds for a little while, I never deviated from my belief that rugby was first and foremost a handling code where moving the ball was what mattered. I always felt comfortable with it in hand but, the one and only time I played at Wembley, nerves inhibited my natural game and if I have one regret – despite the joy of victory on the day – it was that I compromised my instincts that afternoon. Fear of making a mistake seemed to inhibit most of the players on both sides.

THAT APPEARANCE IN THE Challenge Cup final capped an amazing, record-breaking season for me. I was lucky enough to set some goals and points records for the club and the sport that, amazingly, still stand some fifty or so years later but even with all of that, for me the 1956/57 Cup campaign was the highlight. Not just the final either, the whole run was filled with drama and excitement which just continued to build.

It began at home to Wigan and that draw set the city alight. They were the form side and had won twelve games on the trot and we were only one shy of them so we were guaranteed a Headingley sell out and there were huge expectations that the game would be a classic.

The atmosphere in and around the stadium was as good as I'd ever known it there and on a par with either Cardiff Arms Park or Twickenham for an international. The sides were packed with some of the finest talents of the era, we had a massive respect for one another but that didn't stop the packs tearing into each other with a force that you could hear from yards away. Keith McLellan and I were pitted against Eric Ashton and Ernie Ashcroft in the centres and it was a rare old tussle although cagey early on.

I managed to break the stalemate when Wigan came up with an error on the half-way line. A pass from the play-the-ball went to ground and I managed to dribble the ball to near the posts and touchdown – a legacy of my soccer playing days as a young centre-forward with Gorseinon Thistles, which at one time interested Swansea.

Even before the cheers for my conversion had fully died down, the cherry and whites were back in it, Billy Boston producing one of his storming touchline runs to go in at the corner. Ever-generous in their appreciation for such outstanding wing play, which they thrived on, the Leeds crowd joined the visiting fans in registering their appreciation, the combined noise being amongst the loudest I can remember. We dominated the remainder of the half with Pat Quinn having a couple of strong runs down the left. Wigan lost Dave Bolton through injury but right on half-time they took the lead in spectacular fashion. The move covered virtually the length of the field and was another Boston special as he tore down the touchline, beating all and sundry for a try as good as any I'd ever seen. I still remind him of it whenever he manages to get across to Headingley and I'm not sure anyone else could have scored it. That try must rank as one of his greatest.

The second half was one of the tensest I can remember, with the battle end to end and the noise of the massive crowd, which at times seemed like it was going to encroach onto the pitch, making the atmosphere near unbearable. Billy was again at the heart of the action, bundling Pat into touch with a wonderful tackle after I'd got clear but I managed a surprise drop goal soon after to edge us a point in front. Bernard Poole's break and terrific pass put our young flyer Del Hodgkinson over for what we thought was the crucial score but that only spurred Wigan on to throw everything at us, despite being a man down, and the wonderful Eric Ashton intercepted and forced his way over, with his conversion putting them just ahead. We needed something special and it came from skipper Keith McLellan whose wonderful darting solo effort just saw us home, although there was still time for Eric to miss a penalty five minutes from time that would have taken us to Central Park for a replay. To win such an epic in those circumstances, buoyed us for whatever the remainder of the campaign had in store.

The biggest concern for us in the second round, when we were again fortunate enough to be drawn at home, was the weather rather than our opponents Warrington, who were going through a difficult period. Headingley was covered in thick snow and only a sterling effort from hundreds of fans, who came down with shovels, got the tie played at all. To get the match on, the lines were painted blue to stand out from the snow-covered surface and throughout it the reserves had to sweep them in the face of a blizzard to keep them visible. We rewarded the hardy spectators with a fairly comfortable win and I managed to get over for a near identical try to the one I'd scored against Wigan.

If we'd come out of the hat relatively favourably up until then with matches at Headingley, our luck ran out in the quarter-final when we were sent to a ground where we had a terrible record, Thrum Hall. Few gave us a chance against Halifax, who had knocked us out the year before at the same stage, and we went into the game as definite underdogs. We never quite saw it that way, as we were on the back of a long unbeaten run and confidence was high. Because of the way the match was being built up and the fact that we had set our stall out in the competition, there was talk that the Leeds management should take us away for some intense training, as was often the case for big matches. Fortunately good sense prevailed and we didn't go anywhere, I have never been one for altering a normal, settled routine where it is not necessary, I think that brings extra pressures. Instead, we had it all on to cope with personal requests for tickets for a tie that as soon as it was drawn out looked likely to fill the sloping stadium to its limit. We were told that there was a massive black market, with them re-selling for record amounts and, certainly, I was besieged at work and home by colleagues who couldn't get their hands on one despite being some of the most dedicated Leeds fans. That annoyed and upset us and there was even some suggestion that the match should have been moved to Odsal so that everyone who wanted to be there could get in but Halifax were never likely to give away their advantage.

Of the 26 players on view that cold, typically damp afternoon, over a quarter of us were Welsh but none of that mattered in a torrid opening in a hostile ground that brought a rash of early penalties. Referee Charlie Appleton had all on to stop near warfare breaking out among the forwards. Newport's-own Garfield Owen kicked one from the touchline after we infringed at the play the ball but, unbelievably, I missed from in front of the posts and then another soon after, which could have dented our confidence. It got worse and looked over for us when Ken Traill twice broke through our defence, once by sheer power and then with some lovely footwork, to put us ten points behind and seemingly out of the contest with barely a quarter of it gone.

We needed leadership and guidance to steer us through and thankfully, that was where my co-centre Keith McLellan was at his absolute best and I dare say he never had a better match in a Leeds shirt than he did that afternoon to drag us back into it. I managed a successful penalty and Bernard Poole again showed his terrific ability to fool even the best defences by getting Jack Lendill into the clear and he weaved away for a wonderful try by the posts, which I managed to convert to renew hope at the break.

Straight after it, I got the chance to kick another penalty which brought us to within a point. That revitalised 'Fax and only desperate scrambling defence in the corner kept Harper Daniels out. Our wingers had chances and we were given an opportunity to take the lead when they were penalised at the play the ball, just outside their 25 and a few yards in from touch. I'd kicked many much more difficult goals but, up until that point, few that had meant so much. Normally unaffected by such thoughts, I was momentarily terrified by the prospect of missing. Fortunately, I was never one for taking long to line them up and no sooner had the ball been spotted, I was aiming it at the posts rather than dwelling on the outcome and, thankfully, the ball sailed between them. Gaining the lead not only put the Loiners contingent in the vast crowd into full voice but seemed to galvanise our forwards while the much vaunted Halifax pack visibly wilted, having seen their seemingly unassailable advantage eroded.

Fittingly, our victory was sealed in the very last minute by Captain Marvel when he went half the length of the field for the clinching score, after great work from Harry Street and Del to get him into the clear. Spirit and will had got us through, and we celebrated by belting out our recently adopted theme song when we were back in the dressing room, Harry Lauder's *Keep Right On To The End Of The Road*. We'd heard it playing on the coach one day coming back from an away trip and it just seemed appropriate and caught on.

As I MENTIONED, THE final may have been something of an anti climax apart from the outcome but there had been so much drama on the road that got us there. Our semi-final against Whitehaven at Odsal was equally as fraught and memorable and eventually led to a rule change. It was in the same venue, and at a similar stage of the competition, where I had experienced my most disappointing moment in a Leeds shirt, after Warrington had beaten us there three years earlier to reach Wembley. We were understandably confident, especially after the way we had played to defeat Wigan and Halifax but this time it was different as we were the hot favourites.

As it turned out, the match was the closest of all the games we played during that cup run as the Cumbrian forwards really got amongst us, their tackling and covering back a credit to their determination and resolve. Twice we managed to get the ball wide and on both occasions, George Broughton – who in full flight was so hard to stop – forced his way over in the corner. My trademark hanging pass found its mark for the second, Pat Quinn joining the line for Harry Poole to give George just enough room to do his stuff. Whitehaven seemed undaunted by the occasion, having only been in the professional ranks for a few years, and their full back John McKeown kept them in the contest with his superb place kicking which defied the gusting wind. He'd put them into an early lead with a penalty then followed that up with a fantastic effort from just inside his own half and also converted McMenemy's try from wide out into the near gale to put them a point ahead with half an hour left.

The remaining play may not have been pretty, Whitehaven keeping the ball for something like 40-odd consecutive one man drives from the play the ball in an effort to frustrate us and keep it from our backs, and the tactic seemed like working. We were forced into desperate and frequent defence which was tiring but when we did get possession, they denied us any space with their tigerish tackling which stopped us gaining an overlap or finding a gap despite us trying all our tricks. I even had a drop goal attempt that looked good, pushed away.

I was short with a long range penalty and it looked like it was going to end all square but, with barely five minutes left and our Wembley quest seemingly ending, prop Joe Anderson stole the ball, Harry Street smuggled out a pass and from 35 metres out, dear Jeff Stevenson, who so sadly passed away just before the Grand Final in 2007, put over a drop goal with a speed of thought and execution that caught everyone off guard. Even to this day, some of the Whitehaven players and certainly their fans think that the ball went the wrong side of the posts but the referee had no such doubts and we'd scrapped through to Wembley by a point.

Back in the dressing room, after the long climb back up the Odsal hill through the crowds, we were jubilant, with Stevo the focus of our toasts as the beer flowed. Appropriately, he had borrowed a record player from Geoff Gunney at Hunslet and on it we endlessly played and sang to our adopted theme tune, which the Black Dyke Mills band had played to accompany our arrival onto the field at the start the battle.

WE WORKED HARD TO remain motivated for the next month and, indeed, we had to keep winning to make the championship play-offs but at the back of all our minds from that afternoon of celebration was the impending trip to the Twin Towers. Come the Final, the Leeds management again adopted the sensible approach of not disrupting our routine too much. We travelled down to our base at the Aldenham Lodge Hotel in Radlett the day before the game and I'm sure that being in such an unfamiliar environment for the shortest possible time helped our preparations. No matter what we had been through individually before in our careers, the Challenge Cup final and what it meant to the fans and the team and everything that surrounded it, was like nothing else. We were such a close-knit bunch by then that we were all desperate to win something together and for each other. Another example of the club's foresight and understanding of our position was that they paid for our wives and girlfriends to travel down with the team which was hugely appreciated and, again, a settling factor.

Team manager Ken Dalby was also a huge part of getting us ready and in the right frame of mind. Cleverly, he arranged for one of our final training sessions to take place at Kirkstall because, unlike Headingley where the surface had become hard and dry, the grass down by the Abbey was green and lush like it would be at the Empire Stadium. Championship distractions were ended the week before the Cup final when we lost to Oldham but of more concern were key injuries to Don Robinson, Keith McLellan and George Broughton. All were passed fit and named in the team on the Monday – again a welcome move from Ken to let everyone know in very good time what was expected of them – but little did we know that Robbie had a fractured wrist. Ken kept it secret and left the decision to the big man, who defied the pain to play with extra strapping and that proved to be a deciding factor.

It was the same side which had won the semi and our greatest asset was our togetherness and appreciation of each other's talents, although a £38-a-man win bonus helped cement us further!

We were held together by a fantastic captain who epitomised leading by example and got the best out of those around him. Pat Quinn had adapted superbly from being a Union three-quarter to becoming a League full-back but retained the vital ability to link in at precisely the right time. Our wings could not have been more of a contrast but equally effective in their different ways. George Broughton was power and directness while teenager Del Hodgkinson possessed a superb side step and had been a revelation in his first year in the team. The side, like all the best and most successful ones, had a spine of local boys running through it, including in the key half-back roles. Jack Lendill had emigrated with his family to Australia but returned to play for his beloved Leeds and performed so well that he kept World Cup star Gordon Brown out of the side. Jeff Stevenson was a joy to play alongside and just watch; he was the master of his craft, a brilliant footballer who belied his sleight frame. In that cup run, and especially the final, we needed all his guile, strength and assuredness. Fellow Welshman Ernie Hopper and Joe Anderson from Cas were the equal of any props in the competition and Bernard Prior one of the most underrated hookers in the game. He won us a terrific supply of ball against players with bigger reputations. Alongside big Robbie in the second row was Bernard Poole, the architect of so much of our expansive play and behind them, Harry Street brought his vast Test experience to keep it all together up front. In all, eight of the team were Yorkshiremen, five having come through the Leeds schools system of which the club was rightly proud.

Barrow delayed naming their side until the day before the game, which I think was a mistake, and banked heavily on experience with the likes of; Willie Horne, Jimmy Lewthwaite, Frank Castle and Jack Grundy in their ranks. They were among the best around. I was opposite Phil Jackson who was at his peak and, at the time, probably one of the very best centres in the world.

I played golf at Porter's Park Golf Club on the morning of the final as we tried to relax for the occasion, a good omen being Stevo winning the jackpot on the fruit machine there with his first pull. I think he won us some golf balls. At the stadium, I was greeted by my brothers Allan and Cliff, who reminded me that seven years earlier we had all also met up in London, when I played my first game for Wales at Twickenham. The most nerve-racking part was the long walk out and wait while we went through all the formalities with the dignitaries. That ten or so minutes, while the national anthem was also played, seemed to go on forever and standing there just waiting to get started, exaggerated the enormity of the event. The stadium and the expectation weighs heavy. I'd been warned about the 'Wembley nerves' but nothing can truly prepare you for what to expect and I'm not sure either side that afternoon ever really shook them off, I know I didn't. As a result, the team's, and certainly my, natural game was replaced by operating on the basis of safety first.

I felt extremely nervous in the early stages, especially after being caught by Horne near the corner flag, then putting out a poor pass after Stevo had weaved his magic, and missing a penalty. By contrast, Stevo was everywhere and proving to be a constant menace, pushing our forwards into the Barrow quarter where they established dominance. Pat Quinn came up from the back to eventually crash through the cover, the Leeds fans making a tremendous noise as he planted the ball down, but again I was wide with the conversion. George Broughton just hit the corner flag as he tried to dive in and there was enormous relief in our ranks when Lewthwaite went over in the corner just before half-time but his effort was disallowed because of a knock on. We were still clinging on to that 3-0 lead.

During the interval, Ken Dalby told us to keep trying the switch move we worked on endlessly at training and from the first scrum of the second half it came off to perfection. Jack went one way with the Barrow cover chasing him and I took the ball from Stevo and went the other. Wembley's wide space opened in front of me and I sent a pass to Del who brilliantly stepped past Joe Ball on his way to a glorious 40 yard try.

Again I missed the kick and, at 6-0 down, Barrow realised that they had to do something to stay in the game. Horne was superb, kicking a penalty and dictating the play but a mistake put us in seeming control. Barrow fumbled the ball near their own line, and hearing a call, Jack Grundy threw out a pass only to find it was Robbie who had shouted and he powered his way through two tacklers on an unstoppable charge for the line. I was again wayward with the kick. I was never too concerned about goal kicking technique. I always felt that it was something for which you had to have a natural ability and to practice a lot, especially at the beginning of your career. Hopefully, I am remembered for more than being just a competent kicker and, invariably, scoring tries gave me more satisfaction. Missing those kicks did play a part in making this a tense and exciting game right to the end.

At 9-2, we looked all-on winners. But there was to be a late dramatic twist that is still debated in the Furness area. Phil Jackson showed his absolute class getting on the end of a Willie Horne half break to burst clear and around Pat for a super try which Willie converted and with twenty minutes to go, there was just a score between us. Even though we were on the back foot, our defence, brilliantly marshalled by Keith, looked like it could cope with whatever was thrown at us, including the last minute talking point. Horne got youngster Johnny Rea into space through our tiring defence and, as he reached our quarter, he elected to kick for Frank Castle but in a straight race for Challenge Cup glory George Broughton just beat him to the ball and their last chance was gone.

Most of the post-game analysis among the Barrow fans and the press, in particular, was that if Rea had passed not kicked, Frank – who was moving to the inside – would have scored. I was the nearest chaser to Johnny and clearly gaining and, in my opinion, he did the right thing to kick, correctly thinking he was covered. I am convinced I would have caught him. Also, the noise was immense, which may have meant he didn't hear Frank's call for the ball but we all clearly heard Pat Quinn shout, "okay Lew, I'll take Castle", which may well have influenced Johnny further. Whatever, there was no doubt among the Leeds players that we would have snuffed out either option.

Despite their despair at the final whistle almost immediately afterwards, the distraught Barrow players took defeat superbly and without complaint as the Leeds crowd went wild in celebration. We felt we were the better side over the course of the game and chaired a bloodied Keith McLellan around the ground as he joyfully hoisted the cup. Stevo deservedly became the first Leeds player to win the Lance Todd trophy, having tormented the Barrow defence in the first half and cover tackling magnificently in the second to keep us in the contest. Robbie was superb, especially when it was revealed afterwards that he shouldn't have played and Del belied his young years to take his one clear chance magnificently.

Although I would have liked to have played better individually, I felt part of a terrific team effort that had come through one of the toughest possible runs to claim the big prize. I got some criticism from people who had expected the big Wembley spaces to be my stage and expected me to dominate with some flamboyant rugby but I felt I'd contributed to the success.

There was absolute joy at the evening's celebration with our loved ones, club officials and guests when we brought the silverware back to the hotel and similar scenes when thousands congregated in the Town Hall square as we paraded it back through the city the next day on an open-topped coach. The Lord Mayor, despite being a Hunslet fan, gave us a civic reception and I am eternally grateful that I played and won at Wembley for Leeds.

THE 1956/7 SEASON WAS immensely memorable for me as I managed to re-write the record books, becoming the first player in the code to post over 500 points, in all matches, during a campaign. That was principally down to my goal kicking, although the irony of the Cup Final being one of only two matches that year I played in where I didn't score was not lost on everyone, including me. To surpass another legendary Welshman Jim Sullivan's seasonal total for Wigan is something I am still immensely proud of. I know the game has changed and less matches are played now, so to think my place in history could last forever is almost incomprehensible and was not something I ever considered at the time. I actually passed Jim's landmark at St Helens of all places – where he was club coach – but whilst playing for Great Britain, who he was managing at the time, a day before my 25th birthday, so that was some present.

DEREK HALLAS
CENTRE 1958-1962

BORN 25 May 1933
SIGNED From Keighley
LEEDS CAREER 135 appearances, 60 tries, 18 goals
HONOURS Championship 1961; 2 Great Britain caps, 5 Yorkshire appearances
LEFT Joined Keighley, 1962

Derek Hallas cemented a place in Leeds Rugby League folklore with two tries in the 1961 Championship final victory over Warrington. Developing his rugby league skills at school, he began his senior career at Roundhay Rugby Union club, winning Yorkshire representative honours, before switching codes. Impressing at Keighley, Derek joined Leeds as a replacement for Australian Test centre Keith McLellan in 1958. Of his 60 tries for the club, 21 came in the 1960/61 title winning season, when he played in his only final for the Loiners. By then he had developed a devastating partnership with Springbok winger Wilf Rosenberg, the impeccable service he gave enabling the 'flying dentist' to break the club's post war seasonal try scoring record. After briefly returning to Keighley, he went on to play for Australian side Parramatta before retiring and returning home.

Leeds 25 v Warrington 10

Championship final
Saturday 20 May 1961

Odsal Stadium, Bradford
Attendance 52,177

Leeds finally capture the 'holy grail' after a near 70 year wait, Lewis Jones and Don Robinson becoming the first from the club to hold cup and title winner's medals

Teams

Ken Thornett	1	Eric Fraser (captain)
Wilf Rosenberg	2	Brian Bevan
Derek Hallas	3	Jim Challinor
Vince Hattee	4	Joe Pickavance
Eddie Ratcliffe	5	Terry O'Grady
Lewis Jones (captain)	6	Bobby Greenough
Colin Evans	7	Jack Edwards
Don Robinson	8	Alistair Brindle
Barry Simms	9	William Harper
Trevor Whitehead	10	Jack Arkwright
Jack Fairbank	11	Laurie Gilfedder
Dennis Goodwin	12	Harry Major
Brian Shaw	13	Albert Naughton
Fairbank, Evans, Hallas 2 Jones	Tries	Challinor 2
Jones 5	Goals	Gilfedder 2

Referee: Ronnie Gelder (Wilmslow)

FOR THE FIRST TIME IN the club's history, in 1961 Leeds finished top of the league after the regular season's gruelling 36 matches, losing only six. Near impregnable at home, they finished five points clear of the chasing pack. Despite such consistency, they went into the Play-offs as underdogs, and as the sole Yorkshire representatives. Having disposed of a star-studded St Helens outfit to qualify for their sixth Championship decider – the other five ending in defeat and most of them by narrow, heartbreaking margins – rugged Warrington stood in Leeds' way of the ultimate glory.

A classic centre who did a superb job protecting and feeding his winger, Derek Hallas's finest hour came on that never-to-be-forgotten May afternoon in Bradford. Here he recalls his arrival at big city club Leeds and what the achievement meant to that special side. He describes what it was like playing outside the mercurial Lewis Jones and how no-one took liberties with a forward like 'farmer' Jack Fairbank.

Arguably the most famous game in the club's illustrious history, the 1961 Championship final brought a result that saw Loiners' fans of all ages openly weeping on the cavernous Odsal terraces come the final whistle.

IT'S COMING UP TO 50 years since we finally claimed the Championship but fans still ask me about that unforgettable day when we defeated Warrington in the final. I still enjoy reminiscing about the occasion but I also take the opportunity to remind them of the quality of our late semi-final win against St Helens at Headingley. Everyone wrote us off even though we finished top of the tree in a massive turnaround in form.

It was special playing for Leeds, they were the biggest club in rugby league, professionally run and you had to behave yourself, there were always standards to adhere to. When we played away, the team sheet went up and underlined in red at the bottom it would say 'blazers must be worn'. The club badge was on the breast pocket and it carried the city's Coat of Arms; it really meant something to be awarded one. I felt special when I got my club blazer from Rawcliffes. I also discovered it brought unexpected perks because wearing it in town to go shopping guaranteed a discount!

Benefits aside, there was discipline at Headingley as second row forward Jack Fairbank discovered once before an away match in Lancashire. We always met for a pre-match meal and collected Jack, who was a farmer near Halifax, on the way over the Pennines. One time, he was there waiting for the bus having come straight from work and was wearing his donkey jacket, flat cap and Wellington boots. Team manager Joe Warham was not impressed and told Jack that he was not required as he wasn't dressed correctly. I wonder whether that would happen today?

But Jack got off the bus and learned his lesson. We were quick to take the mickey out of him even though we really wanted him in the side.

Headingley was a wonderful stadium to play at. When we ran out, down the old concrete ramp in the corner, you got some speed up and looking around the stadium, seeing the crowd was terrific. It was a very wide pitch, unlike some we used to play at, and that encouraged us to move the ball. Nowadays, I look at it and wonder how I ever got across it. Hopefully Test matches will return there soon on a regular basis because it serves up such a wonderful atmosphere and is steeped in history.

I first played rugby league at Hunslet Carr School. In fact, all games on the school concourse were with a rugby ball. The only time we had a soccer ball was when we played netball with the girls. In one game called Hurly Burly there were mats at either end of the hall. Obstacles, which included a piano in the corner, were placed in the way and the idea was to get the ball on to the opposite mat. The only rule was no kicking, so you ran and passed, which were great basic skills for League.

I was lucky because after the Second World War a number of male teachers who were fans of the sport returned home and encouraged us to play, so my game developed. At the same time, I regularly watched our local team Hunslet, with my father, at Parkside. My heroes were full back Jack Walkington, centres Syd Rookes and Cyril Morrell and scrum half Billy Thornton and chaps would pass me over the crowd to be at the front to watch my heroes. One game I'll always remember was Hunslet versus Widnes in a tight two-legged Challenge Cup first round tie in the 1947/48 season. After a 5-3 win apiece, Hunslet got the all-important try in a 3-0 replay win.

At junior level, I played on a Wednesday and Saturday. We had no bags to carry kit in; you just had your shirt and football boots slung around your neck. From school I went along to Hunslet Supporters and Geoff Gunney, who became such a legend at Parkside, was in the team. I could have joined Leigh, they were going to give me a job over there, but I knew it was not for me. Then, suddenly, I switched codes. My father knew George Todd, who'd played stand off for Hunslet in the Challenge Cup final win over Widnes in 1934. He coached at Roundhay Rugby Union club and somehow persuaded me to join them. One day, Headingley rang me at work. They were a bigger club and wanted me to come across to them. I was flattered but Roundhay had been good to me so I declined.

It was difficult to adjust because Rugby Union was nothing like what I'd been used to. In League there were so many tough battles and the contact was that much harder. Often the referee would say, "I saw that, you can have one back" and you'd look for the smallest player on the opposition side. Frequently the poor scrum half would get it, making it twelve-a-side for a while. After a game I'd get into the hot bath and, after one of the lads had inevitably pushed you down under the water for a joke, I was sore and stung like hell. I'd come home from a League match black and blue. Fans who gave us stick didn't see the sore ribs or skin missing from hips and elbows. I didn't think I'd make it but I got used to it and developed well.

At the time I was about to start my National Service I received an offer to join Keighley, which was ideal. My girlfriend then, who is now my wife, and I were saving up to get married so the signing-on fee came in very handy. I was based in Woking with the Military Police and played Rugby Union for the Royal Signals. They had a cracking side which included the great Billy Boston but, like a number of the lads, I'd rather have played Rugby League. However, there was no alternative and the only match we lost during my two-year stint was at Roundhay.

After the army, I started playing for Keighley. We had a fine side with several good, young backs but our forwards tended to run out of steam. On our day, though, we were capable of giving anyone a game and always looked forward to playing Leeds. That was the big game and one year we beat them at Headingley. I scored a hat-trick and thought Christmas had come early. Our supporters certainly enjoyed that victory.

Growing up in Hunslet there was fierce rivalry with Leeds so I was doubly delighted but I soon had to change my outlook. Leeds were a big club but inconsistent and when Australian centre Keith McLellan left, they came in for me. Keighley was a smashing club, I enjoyed my time at Lawkholme Lane but when the chairman said Leeds wanted to sign me, the opportunity was too great to turn down. I was pleased for Keighley; they gave me a start and got a financial reward. The Loiners officials came to my house on a Friday and the following afternoon I made my debut. It was a very cold day at Leigh in January 1959 and we won 16-11. In front of the main stand, the ground was like concrete so nearly all the action took place in the 'sunny' soft part. I played centre to Garry Hemingway, who got two tries. International, Gordon Brown was stand off, he scored and so did I, which was a good start. We finished the season mid-table, winning and losing 19 games, which summed Leeds up at the time.

Everything was much bigger at Leeds compared to what I'd been used to and significant changes were occurring. Other new arrivals around that time included Welsh international forward Russell Robins from Pontypridd and Springbok centre Wilf Rosenberg. When Wilf arrived with such a reputation, the expectations on me became less but it crossed my mind where I'd play. That sorted itself out after a few games when Joe Warham moved Wilf, who had struggled for form, to right wing. I played centre to him; we hit it off and never looked back. We had a terrific partnership; he was some player and just loved scoring tries. Leeds were gradually building a team that was capable of mounting a genuine challenge for the Championship. Before I'd arrived they had just won the Yorkshire Cup that season, including defeating Keighley in the second round, I'd joined a club with big plans.

We trained two nights a week, three if there was a big game. Doc Adams organised circuit training, which was hard but great. The South Stand had a cinder track underneath it and we did a lot of sprinting. Combining work and Rugby League was a way of life then, players worked hard during the week and Saturday afternoon was something of a release, so you had to keep your wits about you. Matches at Dewsbury, Castleford and

Featherstone Rovers were fierce encounters because of the local rivalries. Facing some of the Lancashire teams was easier in some ways but St Helens, Wigan and Swinton always had tough teams.

THE 1959/60 SEASON WAS one of transition but the team was gradually starting to knit together. Yet again Wigan knocked us out of the Challenge Cup – that happened to me on three consecutive occasions against them in that competition – but our defeat in 1960 was the start of a run of form as we finished the season on a high, winning ten out of eleven games in the final two months of a difficult campaign. Throughout, the Leeds fans were fantastic. What I liked most about them was that when a new player joined, if they struggled in the early games, the fans gave them a leeway to improve. Leeds is not an easy club to play for, expectations are high. At Keighley the fans hoped you'd play well but with Leeds it was a given and on a different scale.

At the start of our 1960/61 campaign, there were no wild predictions of winning the Championship even though we got off to a flyer, winning all but two of our league matches before December. We managed to maintain that form but we gained little credit from critics even though we lost just six matches in 36 games, the lowest in the club's history, to finish top of the table for the first time. We'd secured that by the time we defeated Wakefield Trinity in the final game to dump them out of the top-four play off positions. But even that failed to impress our knockers. It was hardly our fault; the fixtures were split into a Yorkshire and Lancashire League with a few cross-county games making up the campaign. We had played some of the so-called better sides but rugby commentators still thought we had benefited from an easy fixture list and were in a false position. There is nothing like winning to generate confidence, though, and we knew we could take any team on when we clicked. Come the play offs we were ready to prove our worth to the big hitters from across the Pennines.

In the semi-finals, we faced Challenge Cup finalists St Helens, a week away from Wembley, and were instantly written off by the pundits. Saints had the likes of full back Austin Rhodes, wingers Tom Van Vollenhaven and Mick Sullivan, half back Alex Murphy and loose forward Vince Karalius; they were full of internationals and confident but we were ready for them. Jack Fairbank made sure the Saints forwards knew we meant business from the first scrum. Jack told his opponents straight that if they got in his way they'd miss the big day in the capital. Whether it worked or not, who knows, but if I'd have been in Saints' pack his warning would have crossed my mind when Jack charged in. Lewis Jones was in fine form that afternoon and rang rings around Murphy.

We were 8-4 up late in the second half but under constant pressure, they even had a try disallowed, but we had one piece of magic left. Suddenly, we created space; Barry Simms and Colin Evans combined and I got the ball as Sullivan closed in on me. Normally he was a superb crash tackler but I had time to get my pass away to Wilf, some 40-yards out. He shot down the wing away from the cover and with only Austin Rhodes to beat. For some reason the Saints full back chose to try and shoulder charge him into touch but missed and Wilf, in his characteristic style, dived over in the corner with Sullivan holding onto his ankles for one of the great Headingley tries. Wilf always said it was his most important touchdown for Leeds because it put us in the final. That was it, 11-4 and the crowd went wild. The Loiners fans loved Wilf; he was a huge favourite. He could fly and that was his best ever season, he was magnificent. We all covered for each other against Saints, tackled for our lives and deserved our victory.

Even beating St Helens didn't change the critics' minds who again wrote us off for the final. They said, 'wait until you play Warrington', they were sure they'd find us out. Away from Wilderspool, Warrington had defeated numerous top sides, whereas if we'd struggled at all, it was on our travels from Headingley. We could understand why they were the favourites but this was a one-off clash and it held few fears. We were on £35 a man for the final which was actually less than for winning the semi. A club official said to me, "we don't want to spoil you, Derek!" Warrington received £35 a player for their win over Swinton but were rumoured to be on £50 for the final. But that game was never about money, it was only about winning and being part of the first Leeds side to win the title.

We had a brilliant team, full of fantastic players. Ken Thornett was a wonderful attacking full back. He had the safest pair of hands I've ever seen. Wilf was fearless and a great finisher and Eddie Ratcliffe one of those players who might struggle against a poorer winger but then tackle the likes of Tom Van Vollenhaven or Brian Bevan out of a game. Vince Hattee, who was in for the injured Fred Pickup, was my centre partner and our job was simple, to get the guys outside us a quick pass so they'd be away. Our half-backs were a terrific combination. Colin Evans was a tremendous scrum half. Tough too, and there was no-one quite like Lewis Jones. Skipper of the side, Lewis was an enigma. Before a game, he'd have a sly cigarette in the shower, come in, pick up the ball and be halfway through the dressing room before you knew it. There was no big speech from the skipper about how we were going to get into them today and so on and there was also no great pre-match analysis. Lewis would pick up the ball, say "let's go lads", and that was it. Nobody played the game like him; he was so unpredictable.

When I first arrived, I found it difficult to read him but soon learnt. Lewis always gave you a chance to get into space. Out of nothing, he'd slip you though a gap with an outrageous pass. One routine that worked on many occasions saw Lewis hang the ball out, Colin Evans would run around him, pass to Ken Thornett on the burst and either Wilf or I would follow through the gap to score.

In the pack we had plenty of power. Props Don Robinson and Trevor Whitehead and hooker Barry Simms were incredibly hard but good foot-ballers. Jack Fairbank and Denis Goodwin let nothing through in the second row and combined well with Brian Shaw, who'd joined us from Hunslet before the Challenge Cup deadline for a world record fee and soon proved his worth. Jack was powerful, could pass and was the enforcer in a game. If an opponent was giving you a hard time, a quick word with Jack and it was problem solved. Your opponent was flattened. Opposing players didn't like Jack and in training nobody wanted to play touch and pass against him because he was so committed a competitor. There was great camaraderie and plenty of banter among us, with Jack at the centre of the schoolboy antics. We used the Turkish Baths in Harrogate to relax. Jack would open the steam room door and soak us with a fire hose, throw a freezing towel over us when we were having a nap or push us in the plunge pool. There was lots of fun but we were serious about our ambitions. We played flowing, entertaining rugby and gelled as a team.

There was no big build up for the final. Our preparation was normal. We just met as usual to get the coach to Odsal. Sitting in the dressing room looking at Warrington's team I thought, that's a cracking side. Test full back Eric Fraser created arguably more openings than any other player in his position. They also had internationals Jim Challinor, Laurie Gilfedder and Terry O'Grady. Bobby Greenhough and Jackie Edwards were quick, clever and had scored more tries than any other half back pairing during the season. And one player I was scared stiff of was winger Brian Bevan, the best try poacher in the business – the slightest gap and he was gone. There was plenty of quality and much talk of the forward battle. Warrington had resilience but I still felt it would be our day and we would be going to the civic reception as winners.

We changed quietly, wished each other all the best, came down the long banking of steps into the Odsal bowl and straight onto the pitch. There were no fireworks like now on big occasions but we were absolutely determined to make history.

Warrington were known to be slow starters. We needed to get off to a flyer and did. With Barry Simms cleaning up in the scrum it was one-way traffic. They were never in the game, our forwards got a ton of ball and we could have had 20-odd points by half time if we had taken all our chances.

In the opening minute, Lewis collected a loose ball and sent Vince Hattee through but Eric Fraser just got back to stop him. Lewis was in the thick of the action, directing play one moment, covering the next. Early on, he stopped Gilfedder during a rare Warrington attack but he was just wide with a penalty after a foul by Edwards. We got through the Warrington defensive line a number of times but failed to get on the score board.

Vince went close again, Don Robinson just couldn't take a Barry Simms pass to score but we never lost belief or confidence and when we did finally get over the try line, we grew again. Dennis Goodwin powered through the Warrington cover before sending Jack Fairbank over close to the posts and we were in control. We continued to dominate the scrums but were still too over-eager; Vince, Wilf and even Lewis were guilty of dropping the ball with the line open.

The closest Warrington came to scoring were two penalty attempts by Fraser, one of which hit a post and that was another big boost, we felt our luck was in. Our pressure had to tell and it did just before half time. Ken Thornett, Vince and I drove forward from our own half before Lewis was stopped a yard short. Colin Evans dived over as the Warrington defence scrambled back and Lewis converted. 10-0 was a fair reflection of our dominance and we were pretty confident at half time but Warrington had a reputation for being resilient. We knew we had to start the second half strongly to finish them off. I nearly got a try from the first scrum after the break but was just prevented from grounding the ball. Wilf, Lewis and Trevor Whitehead then all went close. I felt good. I seemed to be winning my personal duel and was eager for as much ball as possible. That confidence paid off with two tries in an unbelievable five minute spell, the most important of my career.

My first score was courtesy of our forwards who were so much on top by then. Brian (Shaw), Dennis (Goodwin) and Trevor (Whitehead) combined magnificently, all I had to do was follow them and I found myself diving over.

Then, Lewis made one of his magical breaks, Ken Thornett linked superbly and I saw the line and went for it. I have a photograph of that try and Alistair Brindle is just behind me. Whenever we meet up at functions, he still says, "one of these days I'll catch you". I wasn't aware of diving for the whitewash or going over the top of Joe Pickervance but no one was going to stop me. Normally, I'd have given the ball on to Wilf but Joe Warham and coach Dai Prosser urged me not to always pass when I could score myself and I went for it. Dai, who took over the coaching role from Joe during the season, was one of the boys and helped develop that vital team spirit. He made the lads feel comfortable. Doing laps round the pitch in training was never popular but if Dai said, "four laps, lads" we'd curse but do it.

The game was over for Warrington. Although Challinor scored two tries, one an interception from halfway in the last 15 minutes, we never felt in danger. Lewis slotted over a penalty between the two scores and then, in the last minute following a Barry Simms break, Lewis ignored my shout for a pass to put me under the posts and scored himself with a great side step before converting to complete a monumental win. My chance of a hat-trick had gone but the result was what mattered. Within a minute of the final whistle, Jack Fairbank lifted Lewis onto his shoulders and carried him to the main stand for the presentation. We may not be remembered as being the greatest side in the club's history but we had made our mark by winning the Championship Trophy for the first time.

It felt terrific. Lewis had a great game, continually bursting through the Warrington defence but Jack Fairbank had also been outstanding. Apart from tackling the life out of Warrington forwards, Jack caused havoc with his orthodox and reverse passes and Warrington could not cope. Another big influence was Barry Simms. In the loose, he was everywhere and he massacred Harper in the scrums which gave us all the possession we needed to show off our talents.

Our critics suddenly gave us praise and we deserved it after our displays against St Helens and Warrington. Our forward power and passing ability opened their eyes. When everything clicked, no-one could compete with us and we timed one of our best displays for when it mattered most. We murdered Warrington in that final and, looking back, I still get emotional because defeating that particular Wire side was something special. To keep Bevan, Fraser, Greenhough and Edwards quiet was some effort but there was never any thought that we would lose. It never crossed our minds.

We had a wonderful season. Losing so few games was tremendous and winning the final after being written off against both St Helens, who went on to win the Challenge Cup, and Warrington was unforgettable. It was a huge thrill, even more so because we proved everyone wrong. We dedicated the Championship win to chairman Rex Proctor, who never saw the conclusion of his hopes for the club as he had been tragically killed in a motor accident in South Wales a few weeks earlier. He was a great man.

On the Sunday, we left for the Civic Hall by open top bus to attend a civic reception. The crowds were terrific around the city centre to City Square where we met the Lord Mayor of Leeds. To continue the celebrations we went to Paris. The players had been the year before so we went back with our wives and had a fabulous few days. On our return we did the rounds at Working Men's Clubs to celebrate with supporters, which was great.

THE FOLLOWING SEASON THE team began to break up. I rejoined Keighley then moved Down Under to Parramatta. I got plenty of stick from the Aussies but learned to adapt and squared one or two accounts! It was a tremendous experience. I had no regrets. After six years, that was it for me. Keighley wanted me to return. They were going to pay me win, lose or draw but I'd had enough as a player. My boots are somewhere between Sydney Harbour and Wellington.

My career is full of wonderful – and sometimes painful – memories. I played during a special era against legends and they became friends for life. I remember Billy Boston knocking me out once at Headingley in a Challenge Cup tie. I was unconscious before I hit the floor. When they carried me off my toes trailed in the mud. After the game, Billy came over to have a cup of tea with me and wanted to know how I was. For two weeks I couldn't chew but we didn't fall out about it. It was a tough contest and Billy had thought, you are not going any further. He'd caught me as I released the ball and – bang – that was it. We had some terrific battles and I still think a great deal of him, my respect never lessened.

There were so many world class opponents. One was legendary St Helens and Great Britain centre Duggie Greenall. Early in my career, a few reports in the papers were saying how good I was and when the time came to face Duggie nearing the end of his time, I thought I'd be the one on top. Duggie quickly put me in my place. After a few minutes, I played the ball after a tackle and for a second I didn't know what had hit me. Shortly after, same thing, he caught me again, I had a thick lip and lashed out at him. At the final whistle, Duggie put his arm around my shoulder, gave me a wry smile and said, "well played, son. Never run with your chin out". I learned a valuable lesson.

I played twice for Great Britain. My debut was against France during the 1960/61 season when I came in for Neil Fox and it went well. We won 27-8 at St Helens. I received £18 and £14 for Leeds' win over Keighley at the same time, in line with club policy, which was terrific. After facing New Zealand as first choice, I got acute appendicitis. By the time I was fit again my international career was over as the tour team had been selected and my chance had gone. It was one of those things. The rest of my career I was very fortunate with injuries.

My only regret was not taking part at Wembley in a showpiece Challenge Cup final. But I made some great friends and had a terrific time. The '61 Leeds team was the best I played in. We could defend but given the chance to exhibit our free-flowing style, we were capable of doing whatever we wanted. Everybody had individual skills but we played as a team. If someone made a half break, there would always be a team-mate there backing them up. That was how I scored in the Championship final, by backing up, not beating three or four players, simply getting on the end of things. For players in my era, it did not get better than winning the Championship. To be part of the first team in Loiners' history to achieve the feat was truly memorable.

TONY CROSBY
HOOKER 1967–1970

BORN   18 February 1938
SIGNED   From York
LEEDS CAREER   118 appearances, 17 tries
HONOURS   Challenge Cup 1968; Championship 1969, runner-up 1970;
Yorkshire Cup 1969
LEFT   Joined Hull Kingston Rovers, November 1970

Tony Crosby arrived at Leeds with no fanfare or major headlines in time for the 1967 Challenge Cup run. Interest that year ended in the semi final courtesy of Featherstone but the following season, he was a key component in Roy Francis' side going one better and picking up the Fattorini-designed silverware. A terrific worker and support player in midfield, he was responsible for supplying constant, consistent, quality ball to arguably the most talented and potent back line in the club's history. He joined a select band of Loiners to hold both cup and championship winner's medals. Coach Francis had the vision to blend his sensational crop of hugely talented local youngsters with a sprinkling of slightly older, hungry professionals from other clubs eager to make a mark on the biggest stage. Bev Risman and Mick Clark fell into that category and so too did Tony Crosby who was plucked from obscurity but in a brief but glorious spell left an indelible mark on Headingley history.

Leeds 11 v Wakefield Trinity 10

Challenge Cup final
Saturday 11 May 1968

Wembley Stadium
Attendance 87,100

Wembley awash as Yorkshire's finest do battle and Don Fox
kicks away the Cup in the most iconic final of all

Teams

Bev Risman	1	Gary Cooper
Alan Smith	2	Ken Hirst
Syd Hynes	3	Ian Brooke
Bernard Watson	4	Gert Coetzer
John Atkinson	5	Ken Batty
Mick Shoebottom	6	Harold Poynton (captain)
Barry Seabourne	7	Ray Owen
Mick Clark (captain)	8	David Jeanes
Tony Crosby	9	George Shepherd
Ken Eyre	10	Don Fox
Bill Ramsey	11	Bob Haigh
Albert Eyre	12	Matt McLeod
Ray Batten	13	David Hawley
John Langley	14	Richard Paley
David Hick	15	Gerry Round
Atkinson (penalty try)	Tries	Hirst 2
Risman 4	Goals	Fox 2

Referee: J. P. Hebblethwaite (York)

SOME INTENSELY MEMORABLE occasions transcend their sport. In rugby league, there have been few, if any, more iconic matches than the 1968 Challenge Cup Final at Wembley. The all-Yorkshire affair between the two leading sides, which contained a host of the code's finest exponents, was set to be a thrilling open affair, like that of Hunslet and Wigan three years before. Wakefield needed to win to complete the double while Leeds were back on the biggest stage for the first time since 1957. The crowds packed the capital and headed for the Twin Towers eagerly anticipating a spectacle. Loiners' 25-4 semi-final demolition of Wigan had been, perhaps, their most complete and thrilling performance for a generation and the wide open Wembley spaces hinted at something extra-special. As it turned out, the match was unforgettable but for entirely opposite reasons.

With most of the fans in or around the stadium and a worldwide television audience on standby, the heavens opened and the 80 minutes that followed became the 'watersplash' final where rugby became almost incidental around a backdrop of thunder, lightening and pools of standing water that produced some truly amazing pictures. Standing up became a skill in itself but the conditions only lent to the drama and one of the most astonishing, unbelievable climaxes to any major contest in any sport. Controversy, like the weather, reigned as first Leeds looked to have won courtesy of a spurious penalty try and then, in the final play, Trinity scored from the re-start by the posts.

With the last kick of the game, Don Fox – the Lance Todd trophy winner for Man of the Match, who had already kicked a sensational conversion from the touch line – was set to take the cup to Belle Vue. Instead, with most Leeds fans and players looking away, he sliced his attempt wide and fell, distraught to his knees, his torment perfectly captured and framed by Eddie Waring's Kenneth Wolstenholmesque comment, which still raises shivers even forty years later of, "he's missed it . . . the poor lad."

BEFORE JOINING THE CLUB, I never thought I'd get the chance to play in a major final and certainly not the Challenge Cup decider at Wembley in front of a full house. Leeds gave me the opportunity at the highest level at a time when they were the best side around and for that I will always be grateful. Our Championship and Yorkshire Cup triumphs were memorable but the Challenge Cup final win over Wakefield Trinity in 1968 was truly unforgettable because of everything that surrounded it. It may not have been a classic in terms of flowing rugby but for sheer drama there was nothing to touch it. My memories of that final from forty years ago have not faded.

I was always into rugby league, I played for St George's School, progressed through York City Boys and then joined Heworth at 15. I was short, quite heavy, in fact a bit of a dumpling, until I was 16 when I left school. All of a sudden, I lost weight and developed but my arrival at York was comical. I received letters from Hull, Hull KR and Halifax, and went to Huddersfield on trial but they played me in the second row rather than hooker, even though I was far too small for that position. When York heard, Bill Riley rushed over on his bike to sign me. He worked as a plumber for the Council. At York, we all knew there would not be that much success but I hoped to develop there.

As a youngster I'd watched York. I didn't have heroes as such but was just delighted to play for my home town club. Unfortunately, a mix up over my age set my career back. I used to joke in the dressing room that I was 21 but it backfired when our trainer – and a sensational rake in his own right – Tommy Harris pulled a few strings for me to get trials with the Great Britain under 23 squad. One night after training, Tommy told me that he needed my birth certificate for administration purposes. Well of course, I had to come clean and admit that I was actually 23. It had never crossed my mind I'd be in a national squad. Tommy was not best pleased and the incident lingered on and actually meant that I could not get a regular first team place. My face did not seem to fit there, though the fans were supportive.

I was about to give up my ambitions to make it in the professional game and was set to rejoin Heworth when other professional clubs started noticing me. It was a confusing time. I was struggling to get a first team spot when Wakefield Trinity made an offer but Tommy said York were building a team and he wanted me to stay. Unexpectedly an opportunity suddenly came to join Leeds in February 1967. Peter Moscatt was returning to Australia so they needed cover for first choice hooker Alan Lockwood.

Everything happened quickly. When Tommy told me, I thought to myself, 'Leeds? I won't bother, they are out of my league' but I was persuaded to train with them and thought afterwards, this is okay. I was now 27 and quickly realised that it would be my one and only big chance to crack it. Leeds had not won anything significant for a few years but I could sense things were starting to happen at Headingley. There were some experienced players in the key positions; Bev Risman, Ray Batten, Mick Clark, in addition to a number of promising youngsters like Syd Hynes, Mick Shoebottom and Barry Seabourne. I was intimidated at first, who wouldn't be, because it was a massive step up from York. I had never experienced anything like it. At Leeds, the lads were pampered, which was so different to what I'd been used to. We had new kits, we were told not to wear socks with holes in and I didn't have to clean my boots. It was a different world.

Coach Roy Francis told me I was second-string hooker behind Alan but I got an opportunity when he picked up a knee injury during a Challenge Cup semi-final defeat to Featherstone Rovers. We'd finished the 1966/67 season top to claim the League Leader's Trophy so entered the Championship play offs as the team to beat. I made my debut against Widnes in a first round clash at Headingley. We won 27-18 before going out to Castleford in the next round, which was a disappointing end to the season. But Leeds had a team full of potential and I realised that was my breakthrough into it.

I still lived in York; we trained two nights a week and, by coincidence, I worked as a lift engineer in Leeds. I'd arrived at Headingley with new boots but Roy called them pit boots. I told him they were my best ones but he said I couldn't wear them and promptly gave me a lighter pair. He also gave me a pair of spikes, something I'd never worn in my life. Training always meant sprinting and at first I kept falling over. It was embarrassing but I kept at it and eventually it did put a couple of yards on. Training was tough. When Roy put us through our paces, we all knew it, especially pre-season but it got easier. We didn't have many set moves; our game was based on speed and we had players that could react to defensive or attacking situations in a game.

Although I'd only just broken into the side, I was already financially better off from playing in the Leeds 'A' team than I'd been in York's first team. By the start of the following season, I was a regular and knew bonus money would come my way. Roy never mentioned winning or losing pay but it hardly mattered, chairman Mr Myerscough would come in before a

Cup game and say, "lads you're on so much today for a win" and I always thought, 'terrific'.

As hooker, you have to get the ball from the scrum, that was my job, pure and simple and the aim was to break even, at worst, against my opposite number. Alongside me I had the leader of the pack Mick Clark and Kenny Eyre who few took liberties with. It was hard work but we got into a pattern. Even though we were renowned as a footballing side, we had some tough blokes in Albert Eyre, Bill Ramsey and Ray Batten. The difference in scrum power from my days at York was tremendous. We were stronger, faster, fitter and all good ball handlers, especially Ray. We faced some tough packs in those days. Bradford Northern, like Wakefield, were hard work and Castleford especially. Cas, and Hull at The Boulevard, were always difficult. I also loved playing at Widnes, Wigan and St Helens because they had the extra battle atmosphere of a Yorkshire/Lancashire clash.

The confidence in the squad was growing. The 'A' team was successful with a lot of local lads coming through and the likes of John Atkinson and Alan Smith moved into the first team ranks at the same time. Roy was building a side with real quality but we needed a major Cup breakthrough to make a statement. I knew we'd come good and as things started to pull together they got easier. At York, if we were beaten, which happened more often than not, we'd be punished in training next time we were in by being made to run round and round the track. It was ridiculous. Roy handled defeat differently. When we lost, he used to say, "right lads, one lap, get a bath, a pint, a pie and we'll see where we went wrong". Roy was dealing with internationals and there was never trouble with any of the lads. At York, there was constant moaning and older lads dictated whether we went home or stayed for a drink. At Leeds, it was so different. Roy ran a tight ship and that was it. There were stars but he controlled it. He was the best coach I played for and was really special. The mix was fantastic and there was great banter.

We were going well in the league and on course to finish top, setting us up nicely for the Championship play offs but we'd failed to land the Yorkshire Cup or BBC2 Floodlit Trophy, which was a disappointment. But we still had to begin our Challenge Cup campaign. The previous two seasons, Leeds had lost at the semi-final stage and it had been over ten years since the club had last won at Wembley but the feeling was growing among us that this could be our year. Just before Christmas, we played Workington. Mr Myerscough travelled to games and made sure the lads were looked after. We lost 7-4 but on our way back he arranged for us to stop at a farmhouse for refreshments. Our coach rolled up and the lads enjoyed a few drinks. There was beer and a case of whiskey. There was terrific spirit in the camp and it had the desired effect on the field. We put things right over the difficult festive period by thumping Wakefield on Boxing Day and then my old club York, who we nilled. That started us on a tremendous run and we didn't lose again until the last league game of the season against the eventual Champions, Wakefield, at Belle Vue. The omens for a cup run were good.

We took the early rounds in our stride beating Liverpool City as expected and cruising past Bramley, before a second half burst saw us beat Oldham. In both the last two matches, we didn't concede a point which showed how well our defence was working and how determined we were. The big game was Wigan at Swinton for a place at Wembley. The match was my first semi-final in any competition. I was nervous because the whole reason I'd joined Leeds was one game away. Wigan had a tremendous side, Billy Boston was a huge threat but we were sensational, everything came together on attack and Atky rounded things off with a classic try. Even for a perfectionist like Roy, it was a near on perfect performance and we were looking forward to repeating it on the biggest stage in front of a worldwide television audience.

REALISING I WOULD BE playing in a Challenge Cup final was a feeling of incredible relief and delight. I was jubilant with the thought of what might be, although it took time to fully sink in and we had a month to wait for the game. We finished top of the league again, to retain the League Leader's Trophy, which was some feat. The Championship play-offs were a big target but Wigan gained revenge for their Challenge Cup humiliation by beating us narrowly in the second round, when I scored our try. It was a bitter blow because the double had been on, but it was a strange game mentally. You don't go into it thinking about the Challenge Cup final but deep down, you can't help but hope you don't get injured and miss the big day.

I'd been to Wembley as a spectator regularly since 1954 when Warrington and Halifax famously drew and the Odsal replay attracted a world record crowd and now it was my turn to experience being at the centre of it. We kept our routine normal during Cup Final week and travelled down a couple of days before the big day. Syd Hynes passed a fitness test on an arm injury enabling Roy to announce the team early and settle everyone. There was no-one else in my position at hooker so I'd felt safe anyway! I'd enjoyed a good season. Roy gave me simple instructions. When the ball had gone, he told me to play solely down the middle of the field as he felt I'd be more productive and he was right. I had a seasonal return of nine tries, which was my highest at Leeds.

Throughout the week, Roy kept us relaxed. I received letters and telegrams from well-wishers including Heworth and my old school St George's. We trained hard at Crystal Palace and enjoyed a night out at the London Palladium where Tom Jones was the headline act. The day before the final, we visited Wembley to walk around the stadium. Previously I'd been through the turnstiles. This time I went to the players' entrance. I was in awe of the whole occasion by the time I got into the middle of the pitch. The trip was well worth it as it helped me settle. Maybe being 28 was an advantage. I was older than most of the lads and still had nerves but other, younger team-mates, were worse. Atky was in a hell of a state, I had to comfort him.

As a team, we felt we had everything; pace, power and experience. Bev Risman at the back was a real steadying influence. He was so reliable and always in the right position when it mattered, not many got past him. I'd played with Alan Smith in the 'A' team and his potential was obvious. He was so strong, had pace and was very hard to stop in full flight whereas John Atkinson on the left wing coasted away. There was not a lot in it but Atky was quicker. Leeds were fortunate to have two international players in the making.

Bernard Watson was a quiet lad, slick and always ready for interceptions whereas Syd Hynes was such a strong player and coming into his prime. He was also a character but Mick Shoebottom was the man when it came to Mickey taking. Alongside scrum half Barry Seabourne they formed a tremendous halfback combination, possibly the greatest that Great Britain has produced. Barry played the sweeper role, getting around the back to gather up the loose balls while Shoey was wholehearted, quick and fearless. He'd tackle anything that moved and was arguably the best stand off of his generation. There was also Alan Hardisty and Roger Millward around but, for me, Shoey was the one.

Roy transformed Mick Clark. He was a strong player, a class act but I always maintain he'd have made a better second rower because in the front row you're tied, writhing and pulling. Mick was a good prop and captain. He led by example. When things weren't going to plan Mick gave the rallying call. Kenny Eyre was unbelievable because he had a turn of pace. In one game, I'll never forget, we'd lost the ball, I was on the floor and when I got up Kenny had tackled the winger. I was amazed because Kenny was supposed to be holding me. I asked him afterwards how a prop could possibly catch a winger. Bill Ramsey was powerful, could open things up and, like Albert Eyre, was a forceful back rower. Albert was not recognised like Bill, who had Great Britain honours, but was quiet and a grafter. Ray Batten was a gifted player, he'd slip a ball as if by magic. You'd think he'd been tackled, go up for the play the ball and it would just pop out somehow.

Wakefield also had plenty of stars especially Neil Fox, who was in the match programme as playing but failed to recover from a groin injury, which was a big blow for Trinity but there were lots of danger men in their ranks like Gary Cooper, Ken Hirst, Gert Coetzer, Harold Poynton, George Shepherd and Don Fox. The night before the game, I slept well even though the biggest day of my rugby league life was ahead. The match was expected to be a classic, between the two best and most entertaining sides around. Even the bookies couldn't split us, they had both teams at 5-4 to win. The Leeds lads were on £100 bonus for the final and it was the same for Trinity, although they were also promised a share of a sizeable bet made by a local businessman which stood to make it £250 a man.

Come the big day, seeing both sets of supporters walking down Wembley Way was a special sight. There had been rain in the morning but when we walked around the pitch, an hour or so before kick off, the surface seemed fine. In the dressing room, we chatted and got prepared. Getting changed increased the tension but I wanted to get on with it. Just before kick off a message came down to the dressing room saying that the heavens had opened but we had no idea what the pitch would be like.

Lining up at the bottom of the tunnel was nerve-racking and then walking out, all of a sudden you hear the Wembley roar. That moment is indescribable. The playing conditions, though, were unbelievable. Our boots sank under the water, supporters were drenched and we could not believe it. While the Grenadier, Coldstream and Irish Guards were playing, groundsmen were forking the pitch to get the excess surface water away but they had an impossible task. Any other match would have been abandoned but we made our way forward to meet the dignitaries including HRH The Duke of Kent.

The conditions made a lottery of the game. It was a brave decision by referee Mr Hebblethwaite to play on but really there was no choice. The final had the two best teams in the competition, both rugby-playing sides, but producing that was impossible, there was no chance of 'flowing' rugby. When the first scrum went down you had to get your head around quickly because the water was so deep in many places on the field. An American company filmed the game and afterwards we saw the match in colour and it looked totally different to the black and white BBC coverage. Water was cascading; it was unbelievable. There were so many scrums because it was near-impossible to hold on to the ball; it was ridiculous. We just seemed to be going from one scrum to another. I heeled 15 out of 18 in the first half but it was unusual because when you played good sides there were normally so few of them. The conditions were such that we just kept collapsing and slipping everywhere. We seemed to spend the whole time capitalising on mistakes rather than play the open game it should have been.

The opening 15 minutes saw us edge ahead through a couple of Bev Risman strikes to one by Fox. Wakefield had not been within 25 yards of our line when Fox kicked ahead and John Atkinson made an error, caused by the weather, trying to stop the ball going into touch 15 yards from our line. Atky palmed the ball back into play as he slid over the touchline. There was no Leeds player in sight as Kenny Hirst kicked on and raced through to our try line to score.

Both teams made countless handling errors. From one of ours, Cooper nearly broke through but the lads stayed calm under pressure. The rain had stopped when suddenly there was another massive cloudburst ten minutes before half time. There was thunder, lightning and heavy rain but we had to get on with it. As we walked off at the break, officials came on to try do something but their big boots were squelching. I thought, 'we're playing in this!'

The groundsmen frantically forked the pitch but they were wasting their time. Abandonment, though, was out of the question, we just had to grind our way through the match. Roy was his usual self in the dressing room and just said, "right lads, let's get our heads together because we can do this. Keep trying to play rugby." But handling was a massive problem. Nevertheless, we felt confident as we went back out.

In the second half, we had to be on our guard. Wakefield carved out a couple of openings with Don Fox to the fore, while Bev made a number of courageous catches under pressure. It was a real battle and both teams were strong in defence. Shoey and Barry Seabourne's passing was superb in the circumstances. It was really tough though as conditions bogged down both sets of half backs.

With time running out we needed a score and struck with a penalty ten minutes from time, Bev deserving enormous credit for being able to kick in those conditions. Then Atky hacked the ball towards the Wakefield try line and raced after it but appeared to be obstructed as he tried to touch down. The referee awarded a penalty try and it is still one of the most contentious calls ever made. It was a brave decision and we were happy to accept it. Seeing the incident later on television, it appeared to me to be the correct one but it's still hotly debated to this day. Bev added the goal to put us 9-7 in front.

Two minutes from time, Harold Poynton was penalised for a stiff-arm tackle. We had a penalty in range. I don't remember wondering, 'how long is remaining?', I just left it to Mick Clark and Bev to decide whether we should go for the two points. All I thought was, 'if we kick the goal the game's over'. Shows what I know!

Bev landed it and we appeared home if not dry because Wakefield needed a converted score with barely a minute left. Mr Hebblethwaite said "last kick" and I was sure we'd have the ball covered as it went to Bernard Watson but it pitched in the mud. Ken Hirst raced in, hacked forward past our cover and galloped over to touchdown by the posts. It was a dramatic, last ditch score. Even if we'd knocked the ball on, the match would have been over but suddenly it looked like our dream had died at the death.

Things had gone well for me in the scrums and I felt throughout that we'd done enough to win the game – until that late, late try out of absolutely nothing. I was stunned because the match should have been over and now I was in absolute shock, trying to come to terms with the realisation that we'd lost. There was no way Don Fox could miss from in front of the posts. We were all distressed as we trooped back behind the try line and I stood under the posts praying to myself.

Don didn't seem to slip as some commentators noted, certainly from my view, but somehow he sliced the ball off the edge of his boot. I was kneeling down plucking the grass and then the crowd roared and Don sank to the floor, absolutely devastated. He had somehow contrived to miss. For us, it was unbelievable. After a spilt second we all jumped in the air, ran up to Don, said "hard luck" and then started to celebrate. BBC commentator Eddie Waring summed up the moment with his immortal words on television, "poooor lad", which has gone down in Challenge Cup folklore.

NEITHER TEAM DESERVED to lose. The pitch bogged down the best footballers in the league but the referee was strong under trying conditions. Bev Risman's penalties ultimately made the difference and he should have won the Lance Todd Trophy but the award had been given to Don with around five minutes remaining. Although traditional to make the announcement then, it was a poor decision. Don had a great game, especially in the first half but those choosing should have waited to the end. The match was too close to call.

The lads were so happy. We'd finally won the Challenge Cup and everyone was making the most of the moment. We hugged each other and there was a feeling of sheer elation as the achievement began to sink in. Mick Clark collected the Cup and after receiving my winner's medal in the Royal Box, I stopped at the bottom of the steps and held it up. My initial thought was 'it's not that big; I've been to hell and back for this!' I asked one of the lads if it was the right medal and they said it was gold. I was absolutely delighted.

Following the lap of honour, back in the dressing room, I felt tremendous relief. We'd been to the brink but won. There were plenty of aches and pains. I was stiff because I'd got a knee in my ribs. I could hardly breathe but that didn't bother me. There were so many smiling faces. Mick took the Cup next door to offer a drink to the Wakefield lads, there was great camaraderie.

Back at the Park Lane Hotel, my back seized up in the shower but I made the celebration dinner. A number of the younger lads went out afterwards but I was in a hell of a state because of my ribs, so stayed behind. Even so, I felt a tremendous sense of fulfilment.

Back in Leeds we went on an open top bus tour of the city before a civic reception hosted by the Lord Mayor. Thousands of fans turned out but I was still in awe of the whole occasion. The build up, the atmosphere, the storm and the missed kick were a lot to take in. It seemed unreal. The rest of the side had been brought to the club as first team players or come through the ranks but I was different. I arrived as a back-up player but had now got a winner's medal in the Challenge Cup at Wembley. I felt as though I was dreaming and had a feeling of disbelief for some time. It was truly Boy's Own stuff.

FINALS HAVE COME AND gone but 1968 has never been forgotten. Every time the BBC shows highlights of previous deciders, Leeds-Wakefield '68 is always up at the top because of that missed conversion.

I'd loved to have played again at Wembley but it was not to be as Castleford and Hull KR knocked us out in the third round in each of my final two seasons at Leeds. We did win the League Leader's Trophy each year I was at Headingley, which showed consistency and went on to win the Championship final against Castleford the following year. The play off run that season was memorable for me because I scored a crucial try in the first round against Oldham when we led by just two points. I struck crucially once more in the semi-final against Salford when again we held a slender lead. The win in the final made it two trophies that season as we'd also won the Yorkshire Cup, again against Cas, who had a strong side.

I had a knee problem and knew my Leeds career was coming to an end in the 1969/70 season. I joined Hull KR but the whole set up, training, everything was poor and I did not stay long. My knee was playing up so I packed the game in but in reality, there was nowhere to go after playing for Leeds. Winning a Challenge Cup winner's medal meant everything to me. I was so fortunate to be part of that side. I enjoyed every day, every game and every season of my Leeds career. Playing in the famous blue and amber was an honour and a privilege.

BILL RAMSEY
SECOND ROW 1967–1974

BORN 27 September 1943
SIGNED From Hunslet
LEEDS CAREER 197 appearances, 39 tries, 7 goals
HONOURS Championship 1969, runner up 1970; Challenge Cup 1968, runner up 1971, 1972; Yorkshire Cup 1968, 1970, 1972, 1973; BBC2 Floodlit Trophy 1970; 9 Great Britain caps; 2 Yorkshire appearances
LEFT Joined Bradford Northern, January 1974

No-one made a mug out of Bill Ramsey. If you wanted to play rugby against him, he'd out-pass you with either a telling short ball or killer long pass. If you decided to do it tough, he'd run the ball in hard and stand toe to toe; either way he was one of the most respected forwards of his era. In a glorious career, he arrived at Leeds as an established star having already graced Wembley with home town Hunslet. The fearsome back rower played in ten finals in blue and amber, winning seven, in a glorious period at Headingley. His range of skills and all-action style were evident on each occasion, never more so than in a blood and thunder Championship final against Castleford in 1969, when he dropped a vital goal.

Leeds 16 v Castleford 14

Championship final
Saturday 24 May 1969

Odsal Stadium, Bradford
Attendance 28,442

Title success, in a match that had everything; individual brilliance,
off-the ball incidents and a truly dramatic ending

Teams

Bev Risman	1	Derek Edwards
Ron Cowan	2	Trevor Briggs
Syd Hynes	3	Keith Howe
Bernard Watson	4	Tony Thomas
John Atkinson	5	Alan Lowndes
Mick Shoebottom	6	Alan Hardisty (captain)
Barry Seabourne (captain)	7	Keith Hepworth
(Sub: John Langley)		
Mick Clark	8	Dennis Hartley
(Sub: David Hick)		
Tony Crosby	9	Clive Dickinson
Ken Eyre	10	John Ward
Mick Joyce	11	Mick Redfearn
Bill Ramsey	12	Brian Lockwood
Ray Batten	13	Malcolm Reilly
		(Sub: Frank Fox)
Cowan, Atkinson	Tries	Dickinson, Hardisty
Risman 4	Goals	Redfearn 3
Ramsey	Drop goals	Hardisty

Referee: W. Thompson (Huddersfield)

CHAMPIONSHIP SUCCESS AT Leeds was like buses, you don't see one for over sixty years and then three come along almost at once. The middle success, on a rain soaked afternoon at Odsal, was virtually internecine warfare as Leeds' players, literally, scrapped for the tag of the undisputed best with derby rivals Castleford. The sides clashed three times in knockout football during the 1968/69 campaign, each meeting becoming ever more brutal with broken bodies making the dressing rooms appear like MASH units. The sides were almost opposites in style; Leeds renowned for their silky moves and devastating threequarters, Cas building their success on the back of one of the meanest and most uncompromising packs around.

A week before their third close encounter, the Glassblowers had won at Wembley and were confident of claiming a historic double while Leeds – who were monopolising the League Leaders' Trophy – needed the ultimate prize as tangible proof that they were the greatest side around. Success in the cavernous bowl would top and tail the sixties for them as Champions and the brutal battle that ensued, narrated here by Bill Ramsey – who stood like a colossus among the carnage – showed how the Loiners could adapt to whatever was thrown at them. It turned out to be a match that had every-thing; individual brilliance, off-the ball incidents and a truly dramatic ending.

THE 1969 LEEDS TEAM had everything and we went out feeling as though we'd win every game. We had players with natural ability who could turn a match with a slick pass, sidestep or defence-spitting kick. Having won the Challenge Cup in '68 – albeit not in ideal circumstances – we came into the following season full of confidence, and lost only three games during the regular season. Finishing top of the league saw us retain the League Leaders' Trophy which was a measure of consistency but, so often, the club had failed to go on and win the actual Championship trophy. We were acutely aware that it had only been at Headingley once and to prove that we were the best side around at the time, we had to win it.

As a lad, I used to watch Hunslet at Parkside. Johnny Whiteley was my favourite player; he was brilliant, captained Hull, could do anything and was tough as old boots. My dad played football and cricket so I don't know where the rugby came from but I got into League at Hunslet Carr School, which had a deep history in the game. I enjoyed all sports and fancied myself as a boxer until I saw Albert Eyre in the ring. I immediately thought, 'I'm not doing this any more'. Albert was a hell of a fighter but turned to rugby league and signed for Keighley. I ended up teaming up with his elder brother Ken, initially at Hunslet and then together at Leeds.

When I left school, I played some games for the Hunslet Supporters under 17's side and, just after my 16th birthday, signed professional up at Parkside. I played a few times for the under 19s and then moved into the second team dressing room, which was a big step up. It was a learning experience playing in the A-team and I was bullied, which happens, and then became part of the first team squad, so left the bullyboys behind. My career developed quickly, Hunslet had a mix of solid pros and youngsters in the first team then and I made my debut against Batley in 1962.

My first full season was very enjoyable and we won the Yorkshire Cup, although I missed the final because of a knee injury. As a Second Division side we went into it as underdogs but we were a confident bunch on the back of good league form which saw us go on and take the title and gain promotion. From there we established ourselves as the last great Hunslet side, reaching Wembley, where we lost out to Wigan in a classic, and finishing runner up to Bradford in another Yorkshire Cup final. Both occasions were truly memorable, if not for the results. Playing in that '65 Cup final was an absolute thrill, especially walking out of the tunnel. The weather was hot, it was a wonderful experience and we put on a tremendous display but just fell short against a terrific, star-studded side.

My performances were noted and I gained selection for Great Britain, which was an honour. I played in a home series win against New Zealand and a Test against France in 1965/66 before making the tour side for Australia and New Zealand at the end of the season. We lost the Ashes 2-1 but the matches were incredibly tough encounters. I was dismissed in the second Test against the Aussies before helping Great Britain win a two-Test series in New Zealand. But it came at a price because a fractured wrist in the final Test in Auckland caused me to miss the entire 1966/67 season.

Returning to action my career took a new direction because Leeds coach Roy Francis enquired about me during the early part of the next campaign and I joined him for a £9,000 fee in December 1967. I'd been in dispute with Hunslet so my transfer came at the right time. Hunslet had some good players but Leeds was a level up again. Joining a new club was a challenge but I was ready for it. I knew I'd learn from being around international quality team-mates and from coming under a different style and become a better player as a result. I made my debut against Keighley at Headingley. We scraped a win but I scored a try, which was pleasing. Leeds were looking for consistency and we found it after Christmas once we'd fully knitted together as a side. The double was on as we finished top again but Wigan ended our title hopes in the play offs. We'd crushed them in the Cup semi-final, in what was almost a complete performance and certainly one of my all time favourite games. I felt I was on my peak form that day at Swinton, I got a try and sent John Atkinson away for a solo effort that is still talked about as being among his best for the club.

So much of what we'd put into practice came off and I felt almost untouchable.

Wembley was a farce, the game should never have been played and, realistically, after half-time it should have been called off. The torrential downpour at the break completely finished the pitch, it was dangerous. Nobody could play any football, the rains spoilt it. I remember one incident when I tackled Ian Brooke as he broke from a scrum and we skidded through water, which was above our boots in places, for around twenty yards; we got absolutely soaked.

We had plenty of confidence but when it came to our final penalty I said to skipper Mick Clark, "let's kick for touch, go with the tackles and it's all over". He thought going for goal would see out time so opted for that. Unexpectedly Bev Risman put it over and all of a sudden we had one last move to defend against. We couldn't believe what happened from the kick off. I was so disappointed to be back behind our posts waiting for Don

Fox's kick. I mentioned to Ken Eyre as we stood there, "second time unlucky, been here twice, lost twice". I didn't look at the conversion which would have won the game for them, I couldn't. I glanced at the ground but Ken told me he'd missed it as he whacked me over the head with his hand in joy. It was victory with a slightly hollow feeling, though. We'd have preferred to have won it playing to our strengths; the match is only really remembered because of the conditions and it was tragic for Don.

I went on to play in three more Challenge Cup finals but with no success. We were hot favourites to defeat Leigh in '71 but our preparation was poor. I fell out with Leeds chairman Jack Myerscough the night before the game. At a team meeting, Mr Myerscough talked about where we'd go with the Cup when we got back to Leeds. I stood up and questioned the sense of discussing celebrations as we hadn't won it yet. He told me that if I interrupted again I wouldn't play in the final, which annoyed me to say the least. On the day, we didn't turn up and went down to a heavy defeat but we were without three key players and referee Billy Thompson had a poor game, sending Syd off. Against Saints the following year, we put in a better performance but conceded a try in the first minute and never recovered. By 1977, having moved up to the front row, I'd joined Widnes and lost again, ironically this time to Leeds. Each occasion was special and unforgettable but Wembley is no place for a losing side.

Back in 1968, the Leeds set up was on a different scale to anything I'd experienced before at club level. The players were professional, they knew when to take it steady and we were well looked after. All of us had our individual routines. I'd get to Headingley ninety minutes before kick-off and just relaxed, talking to the guys about how we were going to play and then take it from there. Roy Francis was a taskmaster, he worked you, worked you again and just when you though you were over it, did it once more. My first pre-season under him was horrendous, he had us running around the cricket ground, sprinting across the rugby pitch, and then jogging along the training field. He worked us hard but training was always interesting. Roy mixed up the sessions, had a different approach and new ideas, he wanted us to be the fittest team in the competition to take advantage of the four tackle rule. He quickly realised that a side needed to be extremely athletic to capitalise on it and he encouraged us to play to our strengths, to use our skills anywhere and everywhere on the field. For one session each week you never saw a ball so when it appeared everyone wanted it. Roy was the first coach I met who put players in spikes to improve their speed. We all became quicker, better and fitter players.

IN THE '68/9 SEASON, OUR problems were off the field as much as on it; we had three coaches. Roy had spent some time with North Sydney over the summer and decided his future lay out there. By December 1968, he'd gone, with all our best wishes. Leeds did the right thing by promoting Jack Nelson who'd done such a terrific job with the 'A' team and many of the local lads in the side had been brought through by him. They liked and respected him and he fully deserved his chance at the top level. Tragically and unexpectedly, he died on Christmas Day before we were due to play Cas, of all teams as it worked out, on the next morning. We were stunned, the whole place was, and Joe Warham had to step into the breach. He'd been around when Leeds had won the Championship for the first and only time eight years earlier. He didn't have to change much, Roy's methods worked, we knew what we were doing – we'd already won the Yorkshire Cup – it was business as usual despite the terrible upset. Castleford gained revenge for their county cup loss when they knocked us out of the Challenge Cup, part of an incredible series of clashes against them which ran through that year.

Again we captured the League Leaders' Trophy as a reward for our consistency and the play off to determine the eventual champion was extended into a sixteen team format. That didn't last because it involved too many matches and first up, with home advantage, we enjoyed an easy win over Oldham. I grabbed a try and added another in round two when we overcame Workington, which was a stiffer challenge but we were never really in trouble.

The semi-final was a much tougher encounter as we faced Wembley-bound Salford. They held a narrow half-time lead after two long-range tries from Colin Dixon but we came through more comfortably than the 22-12 score might suggest. Castleford, for whom the double was now on, stood between us and what we felt was rightfully ours.

The pundits couldn't split us, the sides were so well matched and then there was the derby element. There was nothing like the Grand Final coverage the sport gets now but its predecessor was very big news locally. Cas selected the starting line up that had brought them the Challenge Cup and we made a change from our play off semi-final. Ken Eyre, whose experience was vital in what was set to be a huge battle up front, returned in place of young Phil Cookson and Alan Smith failed to recover from a shoulder injury, so Ronnie Cowan kept his spot. The general feeling in the media was that we had a more dangerous three-quarter line and a better kicker in Bev Risman but that Castleford had the stronger pack.

I didn't agree with that assessment. All the time I was at Headingley I kept hearing that the Leeds pack was soft and couldn't match the bigger, harder ones. Cas were the benchmark at that time, which was another motivation for our forwards going into the game. We'd proved it so many times when we were supposed to have been out-muscled and come out on top on the scoreboard but still all we heard was that we had had an easier fixture list and we would be found wanting when it really mattered. Poor packs don't form part of a team that wins the league. We were always up for the challenge and proved it week after week.

Joe organised training for us on the Tuesday, Wednesday and Thursday before the final. It was usual to have extra sessions before a big match and they did not come bigger than this one. I couldn't wait, despite everything I'd done, this was my first crack at the title and there was real determination from everyone connected with the club to see the job through. It was our fifth meeting of the season with Cas, both sides were pretty much at full strength and a lot of talk in the lead up was the hope that the occasion wouldn't be spoilt by old scores being settled – especially after the bruising Challenge Cup tie down at Wheldon Road. All ways round, it promised to be a cracking game.

Castleford were a genuinely tough side – in Dennis Hartley they had one of the hardest props around – and had great players. Alan Hardisty, Keith Hepworth in the halves and Derek Edwards at the back were incredibly skilful but the person I really rated was Malcolm Reilly. The one disappointment in my career was that I didn't play with Malcolm when he destroyed the Aussies on the 1970 Ashes tour. He was one heck of a player and just reaching that peak. We knew full well what a threat he was to our ambitions.

In training, we spent a lot of time working on combinations, moves between the half-backs and the forwards to get the ball out wide to where we had our destroyers. Fast, attacking ball through the hands was our greatest weapon, whatever the conditions be it mud, snow or hard pitches. I've always felt that rugby league is a simple game. You take people out by passing the ball. We liked scoring tries and worked as a unit. Whichever pack got on top, then the key battle would be at stand-off and scrum half.

Hardisty and Hepworth were class but we had Barry Seabourne and Shoey. I played with both pairings during my career and the Leeds boys were the ones for me. Barry was the better scrum half. With the ball in his hands, Barry could always hit you with a 20-yard pass to put you in a gap. It was so easy for him. Barry used to say, "Bill, run at it, hit the gap, I'll hit you" and he did. As for Shoey, he was pure class and the main mickey taker. He was terrific for morale.

Joe selected Barry and Shoey despite doubts over both throughout the build up. Barry had left the field four times during our semi-final against Salford with a dislocated shoulder while Shoey had been in hospital after complaining of double vision. Fortunately, we had a two-week gap between the semi-final and final because of the Challenge Cup showpiece so they had time to recover and be declared ready. The rest also helped others make the line up. It was not surprising that we were carrying knocks as it had been a long, hard season. Mick Clark and Ken Eyre had only done light training and in the final session I dislocated a finger but that was not going to keep me out. David Hick was playing his first game back after breaking a bone in his hand.

There was a lot of hype about Castleford hoping to become the first Yorkshire side in over fifty years to win the double but we planned to have something to say about that. We held a behind-closed-doors players' meeting two days before the game and it went well. We were confident and had the right attitude. Everyone was set and needed to be, Cas played no-nonsense rugby and you had to be ready for a tussle. Joe made it clear that hard tactics within the laws were fine if they brought mishandling or mistakes from the opposition.

I KNEW THE FINAL WOULD be a real derby tussle but inside the opening two minutes, an incident changed my attitude towards the game. Clive Dickinson was caught offside and, from the resulting penalty, we kicked to the corner where I was involved in a move down the short side. Castleford players were queuing up to whack me. That on its own did not surprise me, you'd expect tackles to be flying in during the opening exchanges of a final. What I didn't anticipate was Dennis Hartley, who I'd played with at Hunslet, jumping on my back with his studs. I was taken aback and said to him, "what's this all about, Dennis?".

He replied, "there are no mates today, Bill."

I was happy to play football and to try and beat them through showing we were the better rugby team but it was clear that Cas had come for a fight. I, for one, was ready to take them on along with Ken Eyre and Mick Clark; we decided we'd give them as good as we got.

From a scrum, Hepworth was penalised for feeding and Bev slotted over the penalty to put us ahead but shortly afterwards Cas equalised with a drop goal by Hardisty. As the near-ferocious hits continued, Syd Hynes and Edwards were the first of many to require attention. Ray Batten almost set up a try for us and we looked the more dangerous side.

Quick thinking got us our first try, Hardisty charged down an attempted drop goal from Barry, Tony Thomas dropped the ball and Syd – who wasn't one to shy away from the physical side either – quickly picked it up and shipped a pass to Ronnie Cowan, who made the corner. Bev hit the bar with his conversion attempt but our lead didn't last long. Dickinson scored from close in and we were annoyed with ourselves for conceding a soft try. We had four men round him and he still managed to get the ball down. With Redfearn's goal, Castleford were in front by two.

It got increasingly bad-tempered, Mick Clark left the field for treatment and came back wearing a head guard, Hepworth was carried off after taking a knock and Syd got a caution for obstructing him on his return. This was no game for the faint-hearted. Mick Joyce conceded a penalty, which Redfearn kicked for a 9-5 lead before Barry struck a post with a drop goal. I was then involved in a scuffle with Dickinson and with things threatening to boil over, the referee called both captains together to try and calm the sides down. It didn't make too much difference to us as we were absolutely determined not to be intimidated or pushed around. Approaching half-time, Castleford got a penalty after another infringement, this time by Tony Crosby, to edge six points clear and then struck a post with a further attempt after I was caught for a challenge on Brian Lockwood, which was a let off. Bev got two points back just before we went off to patch up our wounds 11-7 behind.

There was no way Barry could come back because his shoulder had gone again and Mick Clark was the worse for wear. But Malcolm Reilly suffered with concussion after taking a series of blows and couldn't come back either, which was a huge loss for them. He'd been deliberately targeted by us throughout the first half because of his threat. His running game was hard to hold but we found a way of putting a stop to it.

During the interval, Joe Warham discussed how we should counter Castleford's tactics. He made it clear we had to play hard and match them but above all keep calm and let the ball flow. Joe emphasised that cool heads could win the game late on.

Bev got us back into it with a penalty but then Hardisty came up with one of his trademark interceptions from Mick Joyce's pass. Fortunately, Redfearn missed the conversion but we knew a quick response was required to keep us in the match. Shoey almost provided it with a darting run that needed a try-saving tackle from Edwards and, with pressure mounting on their line, I managed to find the space to put over a drop goal that brought us back to within a try. It was something I did occasionally but that was the most important kick of my life. I just felt we had to come away from that attack with something. As the tension boiled over on the field, trouble spread to the terraces but we were only vaguely aware of the police intervening to stop the fighting. We were too involved in our own battle.

We had to push forward but also needed to be on our guard as the minutes ticked by and had a few escapes. Redfearn missed a penalty before Ronnie made a crucial last-ditch tackle to deny Thomas with the line open after Hardisty had set him clear. Frank Fox then almost latched onto a Redfearn high kick but our defence was strong. The Leeds pack put a lot of work in. Mick Joyce was a hell of a player and could tackle all day. He had a big influence in the second half and played really well but we needed one opportunity to steal victory. It came four minutes from time with a devastating counter-attack that Castleford had no answer to.

Bev had struggled with high kicks from Redfearn during the game but his final effort to cause panic in our defence backfired. The ball bounced over Fox and Howe missed it; Shoey and Ken Eyre scrambled it clear from our line, Bev collected near our 25, evaded Hartley and dummied Briggs before cutting inside to race to near the half-way line. I can still see it all in exact detail. From there, to all our amazement on both sides, he produced a second of sheer genius that summed up how he read the game. Seeing John Atkinson free out wide and knowing he probably wasn't going to make it all the way himself, he put in an inch perfect grubber which bounced just beautifully for Atky to gather and sprint clear for the equalising try. That was meat and drink to him, especially in big games. The kick wasn't easy, to the left of the posts, but Bev wasn't going to miss and he calmly edged us home. In the last minute, the realisation got too much for Dennis Hartley, who was sent off after laying out Shoey – not that he cared!

The match went down as one of the most explosive and ferocious finals of all time. Castleford were unlucky to lose Reilly because he'd been the outstanding player in the Challenge Cup final and was threatening to do so again. We took care of him but that did not take anything away from what was a superb win. That all resulted in some bad publicity, not least because of the roughhouse tactics but I still maintain that Castleford set the atmosphere from kick off. As the game progressed, it was unbelievable what referee Billy Thomson let go. Dickinson for starters should have been sent off for kicking. Billy should have been stronger but he let the game go when he needed to get a grip. There were incidents that needed to be penalised, players passed the ball in a tackle and just as they parted with it, got whacked. But "play on" was the call when Billy should have tried to take the bitterness out of the game early on.

Nevertheless, it was a terrific effort by the lads. Every Leeds player played his part in our victory. As Castleford tired, gaps appeared and we eventually turned them over. Our fitness told. All those laps must have helped!

Bev's efforts deservedly brought him the Harry Sunderland trophy. On top of making the winning try, he kicked four of his five attempts at goal, which ultimately proved crucial. It was nice to see reporters make a point that my drop goal had been important, it was always something I was able to do if it was necessary. That victory was among many highlights in my career, I was fortunate to win medals at every club I played for.

FANS AND PUNDITS ALWAYS try and compare different eras but it's impossible to say whether players from our time could perform now and whether the stars of today would have got into our team. It's a different game, players now seem too far apart, wing play is at a premium. As to whether our era was tougher, we undoubtedly had more cheap shots and stiff arms in a game. On the field, you had no friends, only players on your side. I battled with lots of guys over the years but they were the first ones I'd buy a drink for after a game. There was mutual respect.

There were certainly more characters among referees from what I can see now. I cannot imagine Eric Clay saying politely, "come on, Bill. Keep on side and no penalties!" One particular aspect which was better then, in my view, was that the ball seemed to be in and through the hands more. Also, forwards did not get a ten minute rest each half. They talk about the guys today getting tired because of all the games they play but, good God, we used to play Good Friday, Saturday, Monday and sometimes Tuesday as well.

I never wanted to leave Leeds and was upset that in the end I was forced out. I didn't see eye to eye with Rocky Turner after he replaced Joe, who'd always only been a stop-gap appointment. We had different philosophies about the way the game should be played, especially in the forwards. Funnily enough, he coached Cas that afternoon at Odsal. When I went to Bradford, I was absolutely determined that I would prove him wrong and I think I did as I ended my career as one of the few players in the code to have every possible winner's medal in his collection.

ROY DICKINSON
PROP FORWARD 1972–1986

BORN   21 October 1956
SIGNED   For Leeds Colts from school, came through the ranks
LEEDS CAREER 291 appearances, 20 tries
HONOURS   Premiership Trophy 1975; Challenge Cup 1977, 1978;
Yorkshire Cup 1975, 1976, 1978; John Player Trophy runner-up 1983; 2
Great Britain caps, 1 Yorkshire appearance
LEFT   Joined Halifax, 1986

Roy Dickinson's happy-go-lucky nature belied his role as an archetypal go-forward prop, fearlessly taking the ball in and more than willing to do his share of bruising defence; he clearly relished the physical contest. Having supposedly approached Leeds as a 12 year-old for a trial, he made his debut at 17 in 1974 and a year later was catapulted to fame when he played a key role in the Loiners taking the Premiership Trophy. He appeared in seven domestic finals, winning six, earning a reputation as being something of a 'super sub', catapulted off the bench to terrorise tiring defences as he showed twice at Wembley. He is currently in increasing demand as an after dinner speaker on the rugby circuit, regaling appreciative audiences with his tales of derring-do and dirty deeds in typical self-deprecating style.

Leeds 26 v St Helens 11

Premiership Trophy final
Saturday 17 May 1975

Central Park, Wigan
Attendance 14,531

As one of the Three Musketeers, 18 year-old Dickinson helps down
overwhelming favourites St Helens to keep an eight year run of
consecutive silverware alive

Teams

John Holmes	1	Geoff Pimblett
Alan Smith	2	Les Jones
Syd Hynes (captain)	3	Frank Wilson
Les Dyl	4	David Hull
John Atkinson	5	Roy Mathias
Mel Mason	6	John Walsh
Keith Hepworth	7	Jeff Heaton
Roy Dickinson	8	John Warlow
David Ward	9	Tony Karalius
Steve Pitchford	10	John Mantle
Phil Cookson	11	Eric Chisnall
Ray Batten	12	George Nicholls
Bob Haigh	13	Kel Coslett (captain)
David Marshall	14	Eddie Cunningham
Graham Eccles	15	Ken Gwilliam
Mason, Hynes, Smith Atkinson 2	Tries	Jones, Matthias, Heaton
Holmes 2, Marshall 3	Goals	Coslett
Hynes	Drop goals	

Referee: W Thompson (Huddersfield)

HISTORICALLY RENOWNED FOR THEIR cup runs rather than erratic league form – which was often near-invincible at home but could be shocking across the big hill in Lancashire – a glorious eight season run of silverware looked to be coming to an ignominious end in 1975, when the Loiners were knocked out of the Challenge Cup at the semi-final stage by Warrington, at Wigan's Central Park. Barely two months later, they were back at a ground that had so often been their graveyard with a shot at redemption, albeit a long one. Champions St Helens were clear favourites going into the inaugural Premiership Trophy clash and could even afford to leave out Welsh international Mel James from their powerful pack line up.

By contrast, Leeds fielded their youngest-ever front row in a final, with Roy Dickinson one of the three musketeers. Here he recalls the joy of being part of such a star-studded Leeds set up of the time, with most of those around him being heroes he had fervently supported from the terraces, and how – as an almost awe-struck eighteen year old – he helped the blue and amber upset the form book and keep the order for 'Duraglit' going for the Headingley boardroom.

GETTING A RUN IN THE LEEDS first team as a teenager towards the end of the 1974/75 campaign was absolutely fantastic. I was 18, raw and eager, and the season ended on a high as we qualified for the first Premiership Trophy final. That replaced the old Championship play-offs which had been restricted to just the top four clubs. We were the underdogs going into it against a superb St Helens side, but there was a bit of pressure on us as well because Leeds had a long trophy run going and, after our defeat in the Challenge Cup semi-final by Warrington at Central Park, this was our last chance of stopping it coming to an end.

Saints were a formidable outfit and had finished top of the table by some distance but we performed well in the rounds leading to the final. We felt confident, although in my personal battle in the front row we knew we were going to be put under tremendous pressure. I was lining up alongside David Ward and Steve Pitchford, we were the young bucks desperate for a chance – the next generation – and had waited a little while for our opportunity, while we were up against experienced Test trio John Warlow, Tony Karalius and John Mantle. Our average age was something like 21 and theirs was nearer 32 but we were not fazed.

DAD WAS A HUGE LEEDS fan so the club was always part of my life. As a young lad, he regularly took me to Headingley. At first, I used to go along a row knocking seats up and down without watching the game. It took me a while to get into it but I was soon hooked. For birthdays and Christmas, most of my mates got a cricket bat or football kit, I always got a new rugby ball.

One game that always sticks in my memory is the Challenge Cup semi-final at Swinton in 1968 when Leeds thumped Wigan on the way to Wembley. Billy Boston was a star for Wigan but John Atkinson was on song that afternoon and scored a fantastic try. We were going mad on the terraces. I'd been to the 1967 final with school when Featherstone beat Barrow. A year on, I couldn't wait to go with my parents to see the Loiners take on Wakefield Trinity. Leeds won with the last kick of a game that will be talked about forever. The weather ruined the match as a spectacle but I wasn't bothered, I just desperately wanted to be part of such an occasion down the line, although hopefully with less rain on the big day. That game fired my desire and imagination.

I played rugby for Benjamin Gott School and like most forwards fancied myself as a scrum half. When I was twelve, a local newspaper advertised trials at Joe Warham's Leeds Rugby League summer school. I thought, 'this is my big chance', went down but was told I was too young. Joe could tell I was disappointed. He took me around Headingley instead and said he'd let me go into the dressing room at the first home game of the new season. I was impressed; this was definitely the club for me. I was at Wembley again when Leigh beat Leeds in the Challenge Cup final in 1971 and although terribly disappointed, the occasion whetted my appetite even more.

I'd continued to progress, playing for Leeds City and Yorkshire Schools by the age of fifteen. I approached Leeds again but the school leaving age had just been increased to sixteen and the Rugby Football League re-worded the registration rule to say players must be over the compulsory leaving age. But the new rule had yet to go through, so for a short period it was still legitimate for clubs to sign a fifteen-year-old. I was given the green light just before it all changed. Leeds was obviously my preferred choice but Bradford Northern were also interested and with the deadline set, I was due to sign for them until Joe stepped in. I put pen to paper for my boyhood club and was the last to do so before the age limit increased.

I was shell shocked when Leeds took me on. Bradford actually offered more money but my dad said to go to Headingley and I didn't need much persuading, that was where my heart was anyway. There was £500 on the table and a professional contract. Looking back, though, I was conned. Bradford offered a grand and other lads got more at Leeds, but they were the only club I wanted to play for, they knew it and I wasn't complaining. Suddenly, I was alongside all the stars whose autographs I'd queued up to collect and for a happy-go-lucky lad. I was in heaven. I was a step closer to playing in the first team with the likes of Syd Hynes, Alan Smith and John Atkinson. It could not get better.

Initially, I played for the Colts. We got £3 for a win and £1 a loss. In the second team it was £15 a win and £7 a loss. Of my crop in the A-team, I was the only one to make the first team on a regular basis. Some lads went on to play for different clubs and had decent careers in the game, others faded away. It's hard to tell why I achieved my ambition and some of those team mates failed at Leeds. Maybe I stuck at it while they drifted.

Twelve months on from the Leigh final, the first team was involved in the shake-up for trophies again, making the Challenge Cup final. I was still in the Colts but could not afford to go to Wembley, so I watched St Helens beat Leeds on television.

Wally Smith was in charge of the Colts and was a smashing little fellow. He would take the kit home, wash it and his wife would iron it. He'd then put the jerseys on the pegs, cleaned the boots, marked the pitch out and cut the grass. Wally, who is sadly no longer with us, was an old-fashioned type of bloke and a top man.

Roy Francis was a great head coach and so advanced in his techniques, in fact, he was pioneering. Roy used to say, 'the more you handle the ball the better. Take it everywhere – the bus, work and bed'. One day, I was at a bus stop in Kirkstall when Bob Haigh pulled over to offer me a lift to Headingley. I was holding a rugby ball. Bob said, "what are you doing?" I told him Roy had told me to keep the ball with me all the time. Bob laughed, "you haven't fallen for that have you?" I was young and impressionable. I got plenty of ribbing from the lads but I didn't mind. The spirit was fantastic.

I couldn't wait for training on a Tuesday and Thursday and travelled by bus to Headingley after work. Fans find it hard to believe now but training consisted of running around the pitch, some stretches, sprints then touch and pass. That was it, into the club bar for a gallon of beer and a couple of pork pies! For some lads it was a real effort to make the sessions. Prop Mick Harrison was a real character and drove his Ford Fiesta in from Hull after a day's shift. He was a massive lad and would squeeze into his car, motor over and then get out all hunched up. The physio would come over and Mick would say, "I can't run tonight", but after a massage, he'd be okay. Then he'd get back in the car and drive home. Mick was a great prop, one of the best around. I modelled myself on him but with a bit more pace!

I made the first team at seventeen as a substitute against Rochdale Hornets in March '74 and we squeezed home. The side wasn't enjoying the form of previous seasons but I played a few games and it was just great to be a part of things. We knew on a Thursday the squad for the game that weekend and, if I was in, I was jumping. There was a culture on match days, everyone had a different routine. John Holmes always changed late while David Ward would be ready early and raring to go. Some lads put their kit on in a certain order, others sat quietly then would get up and say, "right, that's it, let's go". We'd have a team chat about tactics and run out. That was it. There was no supervised warm up like in the modern game. I was always nervous but once I got my first tackle in, was fine.

On the field, there wasn't really one leader as we knew each other's games so well but John Holmes would dictate play. Atky would shout from the touchline and Wardy was his usual self, encouraging us non-stop. Afterwards the lads had a good drink. Life was great.

BY THE TIME I GOT MY big break during the 1974/5 season, Leeds had been knocked out of every cup competition and were trailing Saints and

Wigan in the league by some way. The side had lost to Warrington in the Challenge cup semi and Mick Harrison suffered a back injury so I was drafted in and enjoyed an extended run in the first team.

We ended the season in third place and although we were unbeaten at home, our away form was poor. The final finishing positions didn't matter much, though, when it came to the Premiership Trophy because the RFL conducted a random draw of sixteen teams, the leading twelve from Division One plus the top four in Division Two. We beat fourth-placed Featherstone Rovers in the first round at Post Office Road and Les Dyl starred, scoring a hat-trick. He was a class centre and almost impossible to hold in his pomp. Castleford were next up at Headingley and Steve Pitchford played a blinder. In fact, we both received rave reviews. We started like a house on fire and probably had the game won in the first half. In the semi-finals, we took on Second Division runners-up Hull Kingston Rovers at home and they tested us. Keith Hepworth was on top form but the match was a real battle and we were grateful that Neil Fox had a rare off day with the boot. But we were through to the final and the dressing room was buzzing afterwards.

We faced St Helens in the decider at Central Park, Wigan, where they had won in their semi. All season we'd struggled in Lancashire, losing six league games and a Floodlit Trophy tie at Saints, but that now counted for nothing. They were favourites and rightly so, as champions, but we felt we'd earned the right to take them on. We had to make changes from the side that beat Rovers, though. Tony Fisher was suspended, not for the first time, and Mick was fit again but Roy Francis kept faith with his young front row and I was in the team. Phil Cookson was available after injury so returned to the second row, Graham Eccles reverted to substitute and David Marshall was on the bench in preference to Chris Sanderson.

The night before the game, I was excited, nervous, frightened and struggled to sleep. St Helens were a hell of a side with bags of experience and I was anxious about how we'd get on. It was my first really big game where all the eyes would be on me but we had massive team spirit and I was ready to get stuck in. There was no fear, we had a team to do the business, including the magnificent John Holmes. He was at full-back then and could do everything; step off either foot, kick, tackle and was as brave as they came. If he was taken out off the ball – which, being the play maker, he so often was – he would just get up and carry on. He was tough but a very quiet man.

The great thing for me was that I was playing alongside my heroes. I'd always admired the dash and verve of John Atkinson, one of the best wingers the game has produced. Once I was alongside him, the only thing that annoyed me was when he kicked on the first tackle. I could have strangled him at times! When you're propping against players like Big Jim Mills – who was bloody hard – and the first chance you think you've got for a reprieve John kicks and it's another scrum, you are less than happy. He got more than his fair share of success from the tactic and always had a wry smile when it worked, despite our protests. His partnership with the Peter Pan of rugby league, Alan Smith – who looks younger now than when he played – was legendary. Both Alan and John were top blokes. I still dine out on a tale about us that happened just after I'd broken into the first team. One night after training, we were the last ones left together soaking in the bath. Two years before I'd been queuing up to get their autographs and now they were telling me about the ways of the world. It's funny how you remember things, but there I was getting advice on how to treat a lady from them! We still laugh about it.

At Leeds, there was always an added incentive when we played in the Cup, by way of a bonus. One time we were on forty quid for a win and club chairman Jack Myerscough came in five minutes before kick off. You could tell he'd had a few whiskeys as he swayed when he announced, "lads you're on a win bonus of £75 today."

Skipper David Ward gave everything in every game and would never lie down. If you cut him in half it would say Leeds. He'd get over-excited at times and never stopped geeing us up but when he heard that, he was ranting. I kept the banter going, they were great times.

ST HELENS' FRONT ROW HAD done it all but we were looking forward to facing them. We had already propped against some top sides and Wardy, in particular, had plenty of big match experience. In the dressing room before the game, Roy Francis discussed Saints' engine room and told the three of us over and over again to, "bang 'em, just bang 'em, get into their faces. They'll get sick of it". Roy was right. From the start, we tore into their front three. At first, they looked intimidating but inside ten minutes, Johnny Warlow had gone off with damaged ribs.

We'd already gone close to scoring when Les Jones just got to Bob Haigh after he had made a long break, set up by Mel Mason and Wardy on halfway and Geoff Pimblett cleared the danger. Saints underestimated Mel and everything he threw at them came off that afternoon, it was his finest performance. He came as a virtual unknown from Barrow and ended up back there but that day at Wigan, he was inspired.

John Holmes got our first points with a penalty and Mel caught Saints off guard with a terrific try, taking Ray Batten's pass and sidestepping Jeff Heaton before touching down behind the posts. Ray was always the master try maker, we were on our way and our confidence quickly grew. We continued to pound them and soon both of their props had gone when John Mantle left the field with a gashed head after around half an hour. Their coach had to make changes and Ken Gwilliam moved to stand off, John Walsh switched to centre, Dave Hull to second row and I found myself propping against George Nicholls and Eric Chisnall. Most of their side was troublesome but the forward pack was Saints' strength, so that disruption worked to our advantage. We were also forced into a change when David Marshall replaced Holmsey who had an arm injury but it seemed to make little difference as we continued to dominate.

In the final five minutes of the first half, we took control of the match with two further tries. Keith Hepworth, who was like having an extra forward and a real character, set up another joker, Syd Hynes, for a drop goal. The best years of my career were with Syd as coach but on the field, he had such strength, skill and was so aggressive, he'd mix it with anyone. Then, from a scrum, Heppy delayed a pass while Mel confused the defence and sent it on to Syd who crossed for a try but had to limp over the line because his hamstring had gone. That brought Graham Eccles into the action. He was as tough as they come and pound for pound, the hardest man I ever played alongside.

Now there was no stopping us. On the stroke of half time Les Dyl sliced through their defence before timing a perfect pass for Atky to hand-off Geoff Pimblett, who was no mug and one of the safest around, to score.

We had a 16-0 lead and walked off to a standing ovation but the job was not done yet. In the dressing room, Roy Francis demanded more of the same and made positional changes. Alan Smith moved infield to replace Syd at centre and Bob Haigh went to right wing. Bob had vision, was hard as nails, fast and strong and you didn't mess with him, wherever he played. We knew Saints would come at us; after all, they'd been 16-2 down against Wigan in their semi-final before going on to win.

We had to be on our guard and our fears were justified. Despite a tremendous tackle by David Marshall, who was another quiet lad but very reliable, on David Hull, Les Jones scored a try in the corner inside two minutes of the re-start, which Kel Coslett converted from the touchline. Dave Marshall was soon in action again to deny Hull when Eddie Cunningham and Frank Wilson sent him away. Saints threw everything at us. Mel, who seemed to be everywhere on attack and defence, stopped Cunningham with a try-saving tackle and David Marshall was again called on, this time to halt Roy Mathias who was always such a handful out wide. Wilson and Kenny Gwilliam went close and all I seemed to be doing was chasing back.

We had to dig deep and Alan Smith at last gave us breathing space when he breezed past Pimblett for a classic try on the hour. That meant he'd come up with the goods in every round and there was no way back for Saints. To their credit, they still pressed and caught us again with scores from Matthais and Jeff Heaton to keep us on our guard. We finally sealed victory with an Atky breakaway special, after Steve Pitchford switched play. Steve is a smashing bloke and was a terrific old style prop with a real turn of pace. Playing alongside him and Wardy in the front row was a pleasure. We looked after each other, always got stuck in and opponents knew when they'd come up against us, we tended to leave them a message. Our graft and bluster was perfectly complimented by Phil Cookson behind us in the back row. Cooky was a nice lad, a gentleman, who was always laughing and liked a drink. He was another who was deceptively fast, loved to chase a bouncing ball and was a good footballer. He ran some terrific lines, mainly off Holmesy and could score from anywhere. He was quick enough to turn out on the wing if necessary.

Come the final whistle, our 26-11 win was St Helens' biggest defeat in six years but none of that concerned us as we jigged our way round in front of our fans with the new cup. In the dressing room afterwards, the feeling was pure elation but I was mentally drained and physically knackered. We believed in ourselves, knew we could do it and now I had a first winner's medal. Looking back at those early games, everyone was so encouraging. Leeds was a family and the craic was always terrific. Behind most pranks were Les Dyl, Neil Hague, Kevin Dick and later Brian Murrell. Sometimes though, it got out of hand, especially when someone put hot stuff in your underpants!

ROY FRANCIS, WHO MASTERMINDED so much at Leeds, left at the end of the season and Syd became player-coach. He would let us get on with it, which was great but if moves didn't come off he'd give you a rollicking. Pre-match, Syd always asked what we thought about the game, which was good because he got feedback. He was definitely in charge but still one of the lads. He had a team that was geared to perform.

From being a young lad I wanted to play in the Challenge Cup final at

Wembley, so to get the opportunity twice under Syd was terrific. In 1977 against Widnes, the final came shortly after Chris Sanderson died following a bad injury at Salford. I saw Syd signal from the sidelines. He came on the field and told us what had happened. Nobody could play on. We showered, got on the bus and it did not sink in for some time. We'd had the Wembley team photograph taken but had it done again. I'd have left it. Chris was a massive motivator for the final, which we won as much for him as for us. I tried to take everything in but it went by too quickly. I was on the bench but that didn't bother me, I was part of the squad and to be substitute in that Leeds team at the time was fantastic. The roar as we walked out of the Wembley tunnel was exactly what I'd hoped. When the game started, I was desperate to get on. Every time someone went down, I thought, "this is it". Then the chance came and I just wanted to get stuck in and not let anyone down. Winning at Wembley was special.

Against Saints the following year I was substitute again. During the build up, we were a bit cocky. Pre-match at the hotel we got together for a chat, which was brief and to the point. Syd said tongue in cheek, "right lads you know what tomorrow is. Some of you have played at Wembley before, some of you will come back again and one or two of you don't deserve to be here but we are going to enjoy ourselves. Now, I'm off for a pint so who's coming?" The door wasn't big enough. There was plenty of singing and drinking, but not over the top. It was great.

They were fantastic times, which I appreciated more when we suffered heartache in a last gasp semi-final defeat to Widnes in 1982. Wembley beckoned but Kieron O'Loughlin touched down a Mick Adams speculative punt that came back off the crossbar with seconds remaining. We were inconsolable in the dressing room afterwards, as were our supporters. The defeat was a massive contrast to the Wembley highs and the closest I'd come to a return. The Challenge Cup generates incredible emotions and I experienced all the highs and lows.

I had immense enjoyment playing for Leeds but medical attention could have been better. In the Colts, we had a bucket and sponge. The bucket would have teeth, fingernails and splashes of blood in it! After a night match, on numerous occasions I sat at Leeds General Infirmary or St James' Hospital with the drunks. I'd be caked in mud with a broken bone or cuts and bruises. Nowadays that doesn't happen and it's for the better. Players were tougher; we accepted it, but at times we played with injuries without knowing it until after an X-ray. The nutritional side in rugby league has also changed for the better. My diet was literally anything. I would have fish and chips at the local chippy on the way to Headingley before a match if I was hungry and then play. I used to enjoy the long away trips. When we'd been to the likes of Workington, we had a good drink afterwards on the journey home. Fortunately, the sport has moved on. English clubs looked at the set up in Australia and players became far fitter.

It's a great sport to watch. I still love the game and admire the modern players. They are lucky and I hope they look after the money they are making. The demise of the likes of Leigh and Oldham with massive tradition is sad but money talks now. Rugby league has moved on and you can only make the best of the era you are involved in. Nowadays, whether present-day forwards would survive the physical punishment off the ball – never mind with it – of my era, I don't know.

The game has cleaned up, which is another good thing. One of the hardest players I faced was Big Jim Mills of Widnes. Smashing bloke, he's a great friend but Jim used to knock me from pillar to post. Off the field, we shook hands and had a pint. The violent stuff sometimes got a bit daft but referees were terrific. Billy Thompson, Mick Norton, god bless him, and Ronnie Campbell were smashing whistle blowers. If you got a crack from someone, Ronnie would say, "leave it lad, you're all right, I've seen what happened". Later he'd give you a tap on your arse and mention "get your own back now". I'd think, 'right yer bugger', then bang and Ronnie would be there with his, "that's, one apiece, end of story. I don't want to see any more". It was a man's game and referees were some of the sport's real characters.

We played hard and team spirit was at the core of everything. Rugby was something I looked forward to every week. I never thought 'I don't want to play' and I'm certain all my team-mates felt the same. I'm sure today's players don't have anything like the fun that we had. Sadly, some of the camaraderie seems to have gone from the game. The Leeds lads from yesteryear still get together and if it's at Headingley we don't get around to watching the game. We're in the bar and that's it, talking about what went on in Blackpool on our end of season break or something similar.

At times, it seems like another life but it was a dream for me to go from Leeds to Yorkshire to Great Britain; everything was progress, stepping-stones. There were so many highs, not least winning trophies and especially the Wembley successes but none of that would have been possible without my big break, in the Premiership Trophy final in '75.

For me, though, the biggest highlight of them all was simply pulling the Leeds RL shirt on. There was no greater thrill.

STEVE PITCHFORD
PROP FORWARD 1970–1983

BORN   6 February 1952
SIGNED   Came through Leeds Intermediates and 'A' team ranks
LEEDS CAREER   326 appearances, 37 tries
HONOURS   Premiership 1975, 1979; Challenge Cup 1977, 1978; Yorkshire Cup 1975, 1976, 1979, 1980; 4 Great Britain caps, 2 Yorkshire appearances
LEFT   Retired but later joined Bramley

At the height of his pomp, in a career which saw him appear in and win eight finals, Leeds fans loved the sight of the 'bionic barrel' taking up the ball. With a low centre of gravity in his squat frame, Steve Pitchford was almost unstoppable when on the charge but was so much more than a mere battering ram, possessing all the handling skills and vision to open out play when it was least expected. He became the first Leeds prop to win the club's Player of the Year award. Arguably his finest campaign was in 1977, when he played a key role in cup victories over Workington and St Helens before taking the Lance Todd trophy in the final at Wembley where, like a bowling ball, he continually skittled the Widnes defenders in front of him. It was a display that took him to a World Cup final.

Leeds 16 v Widnes 7

Challenge Cup final
Saturday 7 May 1977

Wembley
Attendance 80,871

A famous picture of a rampaging Wembley run in 1977 by Steve Pitchford was captioned 'Rhino at large'. Twenty years later Leeds named the team after him!

Teams

Brian Murrell	1	Ray Dutton
Alan Smith	2	Stuart Wright
Niel Hague	3	Mal Aspey
Les Dyl	4	David Eckersley
John Atkinson	5	Dennis O'Neill
John Holmes	6	Eric Hughes
Kevin Dick	7	Reg Bowden
Mick Harrison	8	Bill Ramsey
David Ward	9	Keith Elwell
Steve Pitchford	10	Jim Mills
Graham Eccles	11	Alan Dearden
Phil Cookson	12	Mick Adams
Stan Fearnley	13	Doug Laughton
David Smith	14	Mick George
Roy Dickinson	15	John Foran
Atkinson, Dyl, Dick	Tries	Aspey
Dick 3	Goals	Dutton 2
Dick	Drop goals	

Referee: Vince Moss (Manchester)

TWICE IN THE SEVENTIES the Loiners reached successive Wembley finals, the results coming in pairs. In 1971 there had been ignominious defeat against Leigh in one of the biggest upsets in the competition's history and then a heartbreaking loss to St Helens a year later, when the Loiners rued a missed conversion.

Towards the end of the decade, the glory days returned with a win over Widnes and then success against Saints in a clash that is still revered as being one of the truly great Wembley finals. Before the first matches in the respective couplets, there was tragedy to contend with. A fortnight before going to the capital in the year of decimalisation, talismanic pivot Mick Shoebottom had suffered the grievous head injury that curtailed his glorious career. In 1977, in the closing league fixture of the season, hugely popular scrum half Chris Sanderson lost his life after a seemingly innocuous tackle at Salford.

Leeds' first player/coach Syd Hynes, who announced he'd hung up the boots after the final, had no hesitation in drafting teenager Kevin Dick into the side to make his Challenge Cup debut on the biggest stage in front of over 80,000 fans. Dick's performance grabbed the headlines as he scored an impudent try and four goals, but the Man of the Match award went, unquestionably, to prop Steve Pitchford, whose frequent ball carries into the vaunted Widnes pack knocked the stuffing out of them. One of the game's true characters, here he recalls his great day in the Wembley spotlight, a match for which he will be forever remembered by the blue and amber hordes who thrilled to his rumbustious runs.

THE GREAT THING ABOUT that Leeds side of the late 1970s was the camaraderie. We won and lost together and even now, if we meet up several years later, it's as if we've never been apart. That was the great strength of the squad. Of course we had our personalities, and at times our differences, but first and foremost we were friends who just enjoyed being together even if it was just for training.

We were also encouraged to play, whether we were props or wingers. That started under Roy Francis and Syd Hynes carried it on when he took over. Sometimes going from being a player to a coach is a difficult transition, everything has to change, but with Syd there was so much respect for him that it just seemed natural to listen and try to put his ideas into practice. He had faith in us and knew exactly what we were capable of.

The strength within the group was what enabled us to overcome the loss of hugely popular stand-off Chris Sanderson in the run up to the Cup final. We were absolutely stunned by his death in the closing league fixture of the season, after a seemingly innocuous tackle at Salford. It was such a needless, terrible accident, just when he looked set to play in the biggest game of his career. None of us in the dressing room at half-time could fully believe the news when it was broken to us. We couldn't allow it to affect us but it had a real effect on us. Finishing ninth meant that we missed out on the play-offs and in a way that extra week off before the final did us a bit of a favour because it gave us time to come to terms with what had happened at the Willows.

We'd had a very poor league run and it wasn't until after Christmas that we started putting some results together – at one stage we even looked like getting dragged into the relegation battle. We only had the Challenge Cup to go for but we were known as a good cup side and fancied our chances. We sat down as a group after training one night and made a pledge to really go for it, especially as it had been a while since Leeds had got to Wembley and a number of us hadn't been around then. The more senior blokes were dying to get back there and there were some young lads around the place who listened to their stories of the big day and wanted a chance to sample it.

Two factors in our run were the arrival of Stan Fearnley and a change of skipper with David Ward taking over from John Holmes. Stan really seemed to enjoy coming to Headingley, even though it was for such a short time and he was a good, steadying influence at the back of the pack. He was steeped in the game, fitted in well and was really solid. You knew exactly what you were going to get from him and that was eighty minutes of graft and effort. We got through to the Cup final on the back of some tremendous defence and Stan was a key part of that.

Wardy just loved being the skipper. He took to it like a duck to water and the added responsibility gave his game an extra dimension. Whereas John had been something of a reluctant captain and he preferred to just go out there and play his natural game, David positively thrived on calling the orders. He clearly loved playing for Leeds – he even gets misty-eyed and still talks passionately about it now – and being our leader meant everything to him. His enthusiasm and desire rubbed off, especially for someone like me who played right alongside him and he would never give up. There was no such thing as a lost cause as far as he was concerned and he would have been our Man of the Match in most of the games during our cup run if they had awarded one. There had been talk just before he was appointed that he might be on his way out, so to get a reprieve and then the armband was the making of him and an inspired decision by Syd.

WE STARTED THE CAMPAIGN in straightforward fashion. We weren't troubled too much by Batley – if we'd kicked our goals we'd have beaten them even more convincingly – and then Barrow at home in the opening rounds. Barrow gave us a run for our money in the first half and scored the only two tries against us up until the final but we were always in control. I managed to get over for a try against them as they tired.

The big test came in the quarter-finals when we were drawn away at Workington. It was always hard work going up there in the middle of winter. They didn't give anything away and they played their hearts out. Their pack was big and mean. The old stories they used to tell about the coat hooks being further up the wall in the dressing rooms so that you'd wonder how big they were wasn't far off the truth. The people there were friendly enough but it was one of the most hostile places to go and play. It wasn't entertaining or open, just tough and our only try was scored by Alan Smith in the corner, one of his typical efforts when he bulldozed over from close in. Brian Murrell had to kick the conversion from out of the mud on the touchline and it sailed over. It was probably his best kick ever and we just scraped through but psychologically it was an important win. We were known as a flamboyant side but we'd shown we could hack it in defence at one of the hardest places to play.

We hadn't conceded a try despite the battering in that match and that was something we took into the semi against St Helens at Central Park and it was again what got us through. I've been involved in some terrific games against Saints and most of them have been full of open rugby, like the final the following year, but this was just an endless battle up front. Mick Harrison, Wardy and myself just managed to hold our own against a terrific Saints front row that included the likes of Dave Chisnall and Tony Karalius. For a man of my size I had some fair pace over 30 yards and I liked to try and play a bit of football. Late on and just holding onto a one point lead, John Holmes, of course, started a move in our own quarter. I raced up in support and got my pass away to John Atkinson and, like Alan Smith had produced his speciality from close in against Workington, Atky scorched away from the cover and flew the rest of the field for a wonderful try which was his trademark. As a forward trying to hold up our end, we knew that we had the very best finishers outside us who would make the most of any opportunity they were offered, no matter how slight.

As I've stressed, something else that kept us afloat was that we had a fantastic team spirit; the bulk of us had come through the junior ranks together and we had a fabulous bond. We had power, speed, stealth and guile – all the ingredients – but what kept us going was that we were all very, very good friends and that came right from the top. There was also one person who was an integral part of the set up at Headingley; he used to park your car for you, clean your boots and make sure you were immaculate when you went out to play for Leeds and his name was Arthur Crowder.

We were the underdogs going into the final, Widnes were known as the 'Cup kings' and with good reason as this was their third consecutive Wembley but that didn't bother us. We had a training camp set up at Crystal Palace and went down on the Thursday and had a good session when we got there. We had a jog out on the Friday and then went to Wembley in the afternoon for the traditional look around and, somehow, you could just sense in the squad that the determination for victory was there. It wasn't something that was spoken about but I could just tell. Everyone was saying that Widnes' strength was in the front row, they had some very experienced guys and we were expected to come off second best which was just the sort of challenge I loved to hear. Certainly with big Jim Mills – renowned as the roughest man in the game – Keith Elwell and our former team-mate Bill Ramsey, who'd been such a part of Leeds' success around the time I arrived at the club, we knew exactly what to expect and what they'd be dishing out.

But we had Mick Harrison in our pack and no one ever messed with him; he was a giant of a player and quite simply the hardest man in the game. He could virtually hold the opposition pack up in the scrum on his own and when he hit someone in a tackle, you could hear the breath coming out of them. He was the man we looked to and I never saw anyone get the better of him. Coming off the bench, if he tired, we had Roy Dickinson and he and I were the brash young bucks who'd come through together and just loved testing ourselves. We didn't care about who the opposition were or what reputations they had, we had such a great belief in each other that it was just a matter of whoever came, you knocked them down. Then, in between Mick or Roy and me was Wardy who never ever looked backwards, he was on the front foot all the time as well as being an inspirational leader. 1977 was his year; after being appointed captain, everything fell into place for him and he wasn't going to let leading the team he absolutely loved, on the greatest stage of them all, pass him by.

We had a good balance in the pack, we had the power to move forward and we'd shown that we were capable of battling in the tackle. Behind us, there was Graham Eccles, the best unsung hero that any side could wish for. There were some great second rowers in the game at the time but I doubt one who meant as much to his side as Graham did to us. He was fearless, chopped down anyone who came near him, no matter that they were often bigger than him and never needed to be asked twice to take the ball up. How he didn't get a single representative cap, even for Yorkshire, was beyond us.

Winning meant everything to us and we didn't need any other incentive or motivation but the club were right behind us and we were offered a record bonus of £325 a man to bring back the silverware. I'd been forced to wait for my chance early in my career and, although I'd played in the Premiership final in '75, this was something else and an occasion you couldn't be prepared for. You feel all the hype and tension in the tunnel and can sense the atmosphere coming from the terraces. When you walk out all you can hear is the mass of cheering and the noise just hits you. The wall of blue and amber flags lifts you but once the referee blows the whistle and you kick off, it's down to business. It's a matter of playing the game to the best of your ability, being there to help your mates out and vice versa.

We made a really positive start and anyone who thought Kevin Dick, the teenager who Syd Hynes had drafted into replace poor Chris Sanderson, was going to be a weakness – especially against the great Reggie Bowden – quickly got their answer. What happened to Chris was an absolute tragedy and we were all desperately sorry but Kevin got the chance to come in and we knew he wouldn't let us down. He was a typical cheeky, confident half-back and another of the local lads who were just dying to get a chance to play for the club – and what better introduction to the Cup could there be than playing in the final?

Straight up, Bill Ramsey tried to teach him what was what but Kevin got up from the high tackle and nervelessly just put over the penalty. That was a great settler for us all.

Just after that, we had a try disallowed and it was my fault as I gave a forward pass. As I broke through and beat the defence, there was only Ray Dutton in front of me. I looked across and saw John Atkinson on the wing and he was being covered by Stuart Wright. Being a typical prop forward, I didn't weigh up the options quickly enough. If it had been someone like Holmesy, he would have put in a kick and set them on a foot race which I'm sure Atky would have won. Instead, I planned to knock Ray out of the way which was virtually impossible because he was a great full-back. As I connected with him I decided to throw out the pass and it just went any-where and although John picked it up and went over, he was only going through the motions. It was an opportunity missed.

We then missed a tackle to concede a try and Widnes used all their expe-rience to put us under pressure but we were making ground on the counter attack. I couldn't get enough of the ball to charge back at them and then a magical kick from Holmsey saw John poach the ball out of Stuart Wright's hands for a try that some said was fortunate. That annoyed the boys who'd come up with it for quite a while afterwards. It was actually a move they practised a tremendous amount in training and had worked for us before, luck never came into it.

At half-time we ran off the park and as we hit the dressing room door, everybody as one voice, said, "we've won this game, they can't beat us", even though we were behind 7-5. We could sense that they were tiring, they were older and bigger and it was only an isolated incident where a tackle had been misjudged which led to their try. We knew we had the football ability, patience, will and camaraderie that would see us through. The self same feeling at half-time was present at Wembley again the following year when we were back to defend the trophy. Then, we knew we could beat a tiring St Helens side at their own game by playing football and that's what we did, to perfection.

WIDNES PUT US ON THE back foot at the start of the second half but I helped to get us up the right end with a charge. Then another precision try, fashioned by John Holmes for Les Dyl, put us in front. They made it look so easy from the scrum but, again, it was awareness down to the work they did during the week. It wasn't so much planned as instinct, we'd played together for so long, we were just so comfortable with one another and what each of us was likely to come up with or be capable of doing.

From that moment on we were in charge and were denied a couple of times before Kevin came up with his party piece when he dummied his way over from close in after I'd managed another long run. It was typical Kevin, cocky and brilliant. I said to him as he ran back after kicking the goal, "that's just got you the Lance Todd trophy". I was totally amazed when they came up to me afterwards and said that I had won it. Kevin had a truly marvellous game that day and having watched the match again numerous times since, I still can't believe that he didn't get the individual award.

Even though there was some time left, there was only going to be one winner. We could tell they were rattled when Big Jim tried to do a number on me but Kevin just missed the penalty. After that, we just enjoyed ourselves, as we did when the hooter went. It was a terrific feeling leaping around with your best mates having done the ultimate. In the dressing room afterwards there was a nice and appropriate touch when the management invited Chris's widow, Sally, in to share in the celebrations and Wardy made a little speech saying that we'd done it for Chris – champagne and tears.

After all the celebrations, back at the hotel, the club really looked after us, I got to bed at four o'clock in the morning when the wife came down to drag me upstairs but there was more to come for me.

That game virtually booked my ticket to Australia and my appearances for Great Britain, in the World Cup. Warrington's Tommy Martyn was the first choice and he had to prove his fitness in the last game of the season, the play-off final, but went off injured. When you win the Lance Todd trophy, you get invited to Salford for a dinner dance to be presented with it where the great and the good of rugby league are all there. I went with my father and brother and in walked Reg Parker, our chairman Jack Myerscough and Doc Novis, who was the Leeds medic at the time. Reg said, "you don't know who I am?" and I replied, "I haven't got a clue". Doctor Novis said, "roll up your sleeve," and gave me three injections while Jack Myerscough added "congratulations" and handed over a brown envelope. It wasn't until Reg said, "I want you at Manchester Airport in the morning," that it fully dawned on me what was happening.

As I got up to accept the trophy I was very emotional. I still fill up thinking about it even now. Being selected for your country – wow! I had to apologise to the people there because I had to go home. I met up with David Ward – we hadn't seen each other since the final – John and Les and the rest of the team and went out training. I hadn't done any since the final, because I thought my season was over. I hadn't expected to go to the World Cup.

Like Leeds in the Challenge Cup, we were listed as no hopers over there yet we made the final but just lost out. It was unbelievable and if George Fairbairn had kicked the goal we'd have beaten the Aussies in their own backyard. I loved it and I played in all the Tests and tour games and have the memory of scoring in the World Cup final. Not bad for a lad from Hunslet and East Leeds who some thought couldn't play at the top level.

The key factor in retaining the Challenge Cup in 1978 was that the team stayed together. We had the foreign imports, Mick Harrison and then Mick Crane from Hull, but we'd been a settled bunch for such a long time. We played for each other, socialised together and did everything as a group.

People ask me if I miss it nowadays and I always tell them that I don't because I enjoyed every minute that I was associated with the game. I genuinely hope the same applies to the lads today and they have as much fun as we did. We knew full well what our business was and that was on the field and at training but away from it we had some memorable times. We all loved Thursdays, it was pay day and after that the whole lot of us went out, including the staff, that was the rule.

JOHN ATKINSON
LEFT WING 1965–1982

BORN   3 October 1946
SIGNED   From Roundhay RUFC, May 1965
LEEDS CAREER 518 appearances, 340 tries
HONOURS   Championship 1969, 1972; Premiership 1975, 1979; Challenge Cup 1968, 1977, 1978; Yorkshire Cup 1968, 1970, 1972, 1973, 1975, 1979, 1980; John Player Trophy 1973; BBC2 Floodlit Trophy 1970; 26 Great Britain caps, 11 England caps, 15 Yorkshire appearances
LEFT   Joined Carlisle as Player/Coach

Atky was poetry in motion gliding down the Loiners' left wing in a glorious 18 year career in blue and amber. The ultimate big game player, appearing in 20 finals and a winner on an incredible 16 occasions, he had a dash and panache that that was the very essence of Headingley's entertainment principle. His supreme balance and searing pace which saw him glide past opponents brought him 340 touchdowns, second only in the club's history to the legendary Eric Harris. Renowned for his one armed salute after scoring, he headed the league's seasonal try scoring charts on three occasions. So often 'Johnny on the spot', his brace of touchdowns in the deciding Third Test in Sydney in 1970 was germane to Britain winning the Ashes, a feeling they have not enjoyed since.

Leeds 14 v St Helens 12

Challenge Cup final
Saturday 13 May 1978

Wembley Stadium
Attendance 95,872

Ten points down in as many minutes Leeds stage the then greatest comeback in history in the final of the 'Crown Jewel' competition and one that ranks among the greatest ever seen

Teams

Willie Oulton	1	Geoff Pimblett (captain)
David Smith	2	Les Jones
Neil Hague	3	Derek Noonan
Les Dyl	4	Peter Glynn
John Atkinson	5	Roy Mathais
John Holmes	6	Bill Francis
Sammy Sanderson	7	Ken Gwilliam
Mick Harrison	8	David Chisnall
David Ward (captain)	9	Graham Liptrot
Steve Pitchford	10	Mel James
Graham Eccles	11	George Nicholls
Phil Cookson	12	Eddie Cunningham
Mick Crane	13	Harry Pinner
Kevin Dick	14	Alan Ashton
Roy Dickinson	15	Tony Karalius
Atkinson, Smith, Cookson	Tries	Liptrot, Francis
Oulton	Goals	Pimblett 3
Ward 2, Holmes	Drop Goals	

Referee: W Thompson (Huddersfield)

THE 1978 CHALLENGE CUP final at Wembley ranks as one of the greatest in the history of the 'crown jewel' competition. Ten points down in as many minutes and with their legion of fans inside the Twin Towers with head in hands, the Loiners staged the greatest recovery ever seen to emerge victorious in a frantic finish, turning despair into delirium.

As so often, the tide was turned by a try from John Atkinson as he deliciously turned and tormented St Helens full back Geoff Pimblett to glide over out wide. Here he tells how important playing in the national stadium was to him and how, magnificently led by the incomparable John Holmes – who scandalously missed out on the Lance Todd trophy – Leeds showed immense belief and skill to retain the prized silverware that sun-drenched afternoon.

Even thirty years on, that match up with Saints stands the test of time; two magnificent footballing sides going at each other hammer-and-tongs for the entire eighty minutes and with almost 100,000 fans holding their breath in the final, dramatic denouement.

I WAS FORTUNATE ENOUGH TO play in five Challenge Cup finals for Leeds and all were memorable for different reasons, the occasion always delivered. After the lottery of the 'Watersplash' victory in 1968 against Wakefield, then defeats to Leigh and St Helens in the early 70s, it was thrilling to come back from a bad injury and help defeat Widnes in the '77 final. Walking off at Wembley that afternoon I wondered to myself if I would be back again. As it turned out, I didn't have long to wait and was there again the following season to play Saints in a match that is still talked about for its quality. As I left the arena after that clash I thought, 'even if I don't play here again, I've done everything I set out to do in the game'.

I COME FROM A RUGBY LEAGUE family with a unique record as three generations won Challenge Cup winner's medals playing for Leeds clubs, on the left wing, at Wembley. My grandad, George Broughton senior, was in the Hunslet side that beat Widnes in 1934, Uncle George Broughton was a major part of Leeds' success in 1957 and I continued the tradition. It was inevitable I'd support Leeds but the first match I saw was at Wheldon Road when Uncle George played for Castleford before he moved to Headingley. I was at the Twin Towers with my parents to watch him and dad was a massive Loiners fan. We spent many happy hours talking about great players he saw from the 30s onwards like Vic Hey and Eric Harris.

After experiencing league at Primary School, I played rugby union for West Park Secondary Modern and Moor Grange before joining Roundhay, who were a good club side in the region. I grew up in a sporting era, we weren't allowed to sit in front of a television, and had to be dragged home at night from playing out by our parents. On a weekend, I'd play rugby on a morning and afternoon as well as in midweek.

I played centre up at Chandos Park before dislocating a shoulder and was cautious on my return that it had healed properly, which was how I ended up on the left wing. The second team was short of a winger, so I slotted in and the rest is history. Having made the move, my dad gave me some good advice. He told me to ignore the full back when I broke through and not to make eye contact, that way I'd keep him guessing. I could see the touchline, posts and try line and if I focussed on that and drove forward, I'd beat the full back without actually knowing it.

Rugby league scouts were watching me from various clubs and on one occasion I heard that Arthur Clues was going to be in the crowd. The next thing there was a knock on the door and as my boyhood dream was to play for the Loiners, it was not a difficult decision to sign in May 1965. Roundhay wanted me to stay, they were certain I'd play for Yorkshire and possibly England but I'd grown up watching greats like Lewis Jones and Jeff Stevenson, so Leeds was for me.

Breaking into the first team was hard. In the A-team, Alan Smith on the right wing scored freely but I struggled. Jack Nelson, God bless him, was coach and asked Roy Francis to bring me into the first team dressing room and try me out. I lacked confidence but eventually made my debut in a win against York a year after I'd signed, scoring two tries. In the second team, I seemed like a fish out of water but once I'd made the first team, I felt it was my destiny.

Alan and I broke through on a more regular basis in the 1966/67 season. The squad trained two, sometimes three nights a week but my dad drilled into me that I would not make a top-flight rugby player on two nights only. I'd been a keen sprinter and done other sports so training was second nature, by 1968 I was doing the 100 metres in a time of 10.8 seconds which would have got me a place in the semi finals of that year's Olympics. Fitness was one thing but Roy Francis used to say in his team talk, "you're playing for Leeds because you're good enough, I expect you to take charge out there." We dictated our tactics on the field and, if we had a problem, we adapted.

By now, Leeds had not won a major honour for over a decade but there was a real determination throughout the club to land one and we felt we'd grown the side to achieve it. Everything clicked through the influence of Roy. Some experienced recruits moved the club forward then he built a team around younger players. Our success was down to fitness and pace throughout the side. Everyone had to run to their limit because Roy believed he'd get the best out of a player if they were fit. He expected me to be able to run the length of the pitch at the same pace in the last minute as the first. I lost count of the times we came through late on because of that and I've done more runs on the cricket pitch than Geoff Boycott.

Roy set the ground rules. He would tell you what he wanted but would listen as well, everyone pulled together. All the lads were mickey takers. Tony Fisher went over the top at times when he threw you into a red-hot bath in the dressing room. You'd come out resembling a lobster! Later, Neil Hague and Brian Murrell were terrible together but it built camaraderie and didn't matter if you were a senior or a junior player. We also mixed with the Leeds United lads who were a top side at the time. There was great banter between us and the likes of Billy Bremner, Jack Charlton, Norman Hunter and Paul Reaney. We watched out for each other's results and enjoyed the odd bet. I was quick but 'Speedy' Reaney thought he could outpace me, so arranged a winner-takes-all race at a local dog track. The rugby lads had a good payday!

LIKE ALL PLAYERS, I WANTED to experience playing in a Challenge Cup final. In 1968, we faced Wigan in the semis and although the underdogs, played them off the park. I was only 21 and Bill Ramsey set me up for a great try that in many ways made my reputation. It is still talked of as the best of my Leeds career but a hat-trick against Widnes shortly after the Ashes tour in 1970 took some beating. Dad said two of them were the best he'd seen at Headingley, which was some compliment, but they came in a league game not a high-profile match so were quickly forgotten.

The final with Wakefield was expected to be a classic but it ended up a wash out. The television pictures didn't show how bad it was out there. The Wembley turf was renowned worldwide, it was closely packed and lush but the water wouldn't go through it, it just lay there like a film on top. It was the only match throughout my entire career that I ever came off cleaner than I went on.

For me it was the story of two tries. We led early on then Don Fox kicked 40 yards downfield. I chased back, tried to keep the ball in play, next thing I was in the railings. I looked up and Ken Hirst had touched down. Late on I got a penalty try and 40 years on fans still talk about it. All I remember was fly-kicking a ball and chasing it. The ball was going all over the place because of the water. A Wakefield player impeded me and the referee gave a penalty try. I didn't feel sorry for Don Fox at that moment he missed the shot at goal that would have won it for Trinity, in that dramatic second he was my best friend but it had a massive effect on him and all from a stupid goal kick. I was lying on the grass at the time, I couldn't bring myself to watch. I heard the roar from Leeds supporters and jumped up in the air. It was great, we were victorious and it was my first Wembley medal but I wish we'd have won it in a different way. It was a one-off match that should never have been played and wouldn't have been if it had not been the Cup final.

In 1971, we faced Leigh when Syd Hynes got sent off. It was a terrible decision but we missed the influence of Shoey, Alan Smith and Ray Batten. Before the final, Shoey sustained a head injury that ended his career. It was a tragedy, he was Mr. Dynamite, laughed through everything and was a wonderful footballer. He could tackle, had masses of energy and was so strong. That final was labelled as a huge upset but fans forget Leeds finished third and Leigh fourth that season. They were not a poor side but we failed to perform. Twelve months later, we came up against St Helens. It was an excellent final, two good sides battling it out. We made a dreadful start in the opening minute, battled but eventually lost narrowly.

Before our run to the 1977 final against Widnes, I was out for nine months after breaking a leg and dislocating an ankle against Wigan. It took time getting me to hospital and I was close to losing my leg. The registrar assessed the damage and put my ankle back before seeing to the broken leg. I nearly went through three floors of St James'. I was in plaster up to my thigh for ages. Later, I asked the Doc why he did not put me under first and he said that if there had been any further delay I'd have lost the leg.

I was ten weeks into a police course and after much persuading, permission was granted for me to finish it on crutches. On the last night, whilst joking about, my so-called best friend pinched a crutch; I fell over, broke a wrist and had to have a bone graft in my hand. Fortunately, Doc Adams, who worked at Leeds United, had a clinic at Jimmy's Hospital. His physio was an international hockey player and advised me on rehabilitation. I bought soft walking boots and got permission to run through a field at a local farm. I never had trouble again. I came back for the Challenge Cup run; and we were determined that it would be a good one.

After grinding out a win at Workington, I scored tries against Barrow then Saints in the semi-final as we got back to Wembley. It was a great feeling. We hadn't had a good season in '77; we were struggling quite a lot. The whole group of us went over to the bowling green which is not there now – which is a real shame – prior to the cup run starting. We sat down and talked about the fact that we were a lot better side than we were showing and we had to do something about it. None of us could put a reason on why we were performing badly but we pledged to have a go in the cup because we owed it to the supporters. Things went from good to better and each round we just got stronger right through to the final. Both the finals in '77 and '78 were absolutely first class and don't always get the credit they should do; there was some magnificent rugby shown in them. They were fabulous to play in, although, obviously, winning makes a massive difference. Some came of age, like Kevin Dick and there were such good individual battles especially among the forwards. They were my fourth and fifth trips to the Twin Towers and it was a bit easier to relax because I was in my early 30s and there was nothing much to prove. Being one of the senior guys, unconsciously we played a part in helping the less experienced ones to cope but the younger guys equipped themselves fantastically, they just got on with the job and seemed to enjoy it and that's what you have to do.

I got an undisputed Wembley try against Widnes. Stuart Wright goaded me during the build up, "Atky's over the hill", the usual thing. When John Holmes put a high ball up to the corner, I scored, reaching over Stuart for the ball which was satisfying. A number of journalists said John's kick was 'speculative', a 'lucky bounce' and 'mismanaged by Wright'. It was anything but, it was a planned move; I knew that it was coming, absolutely. We had practiced it and done it many times in matches and I knew for a fact when he looked up, that it was going to happen. If it had been done today, you'd have never kept 'Stevo' and the Sky people quiet, they would have been raving over it. John was such a good kicker that the ball landed exactly where it should have done and, unfortunately for him, Stuart Wright misjudged the accuracy of it which gave me the chance to score.

At a '77 reunion dinner, we watched the final and I couldn't believe the pressure Widnes put us under in the first half but we stood firm. Kevin Dick had a great game. I thought at the time 'if young Kevin can enjoy it and I may never play here again, I had better make the most of the occasion.' My hopes of a return to the capital came true but not before I'd experienced a bad time early in the 1977/78 season. My police shift meant I was playing after coming off nights or getting up at 5am, working and then going to Headingley. It backfired against Wigan in a John Player Trophy tie when Green Vigo roasted me and scored a hat-trick. He did well but I was below par, my preparation was nowhere near ideal. My rota had to change and CID backed my training regime.

Our Challenge Cup run started against lowly Halifax when a stray dog shared the headlines as we won in front of BBC cameras. We overcame Wakefield Trinity at Belle Vue in the mud, which was a terrific result, it was never easy to win there. The quarter final was an epic, at a vibrant Headingley and I was fortunate to grab the limelight with two memorable tries down the North Stand side against Bradford. For the first, from a scrum on our own quarter, Sammy Sanderson nodded to me as he took the ball round to feed it. I knew Dave Barends had been given instructions not to leave his wing and give me the outside but he moved infield slightly when Sammy came round and just as Dave got to him, Sammy slipped me the pass and I had an open field after that.

We reached Wembley after coming from behind against Featherstone Rovers when John Holmes sparked a second half comeback with a great try despite a massive gash in his leg, but that was Holmesy for you. His genius was obvious but his bravery underestimated. He was the complete rugby player but never got the credit he deserved. Subtle and quick, John read the game superbly. Like footballer Bobby Moore he was not the fastest, but was always in the right place at the right time. Fans often said "great try, Atky", but forgot John started it. He was the best Leeds player I performed along-side, just ahead of Shoey. One thing between us never altered, John always gave me a piece of chewing gum as we left the dressing room but I got rid of it before taking the field. I could never play with it.

IN THE FINAL, WE FACED St Helens again and a classic was on the cards in what was another personal landmark, my 400th appearance. The media made a lot of the statistic but for me, winning was all that mattered. Saints started to build up on the Monday and trained in Cobham. We followed our normal routine in Leeds and had a photo call before travelling down on the Thursday. We trained at Crystal Palace and were slight under-dogs, which suited us. Coach Syd Hynes had options. Alan Smith had regained fitness but David Smith had played in the earlier rounds and was top try scorer for the season and Kevin Dick and Roy Dickinson had returned to form but scrum half Sammy Sanderson was playing well and our forwards were solid. Syd selected the team that had played against Featherstone so David was in and Sammy kept his place, leaving Kevin and Roy on the bench. He knew the pair of them could be relied on whatever the state of the game and would make a significant impact when called upon.

I was convinced we had the edge. Full back Willie Oulton was solid and a sound goal kicker. David Smith had bags of pace on the wing and was a great opportunist. At centre, Neil Hague was underrated; you never quite knew what he might do. It surprised opponents when he torpedoed the ball wide but we'd grown up with Neil so generally could read him. Les Dyl, inside me, was awesome; his pace and power was incredible. I used to marvel at Alan Smith and Syd Hynes when they partnered each other. Together they were a force and when Les came into the team, we clicked. I used to tell Les, "go where you want, I'll get there, give me the ball". He did and we scored a stack of tries in tandem. Our supporters were never shy in letting the team know how we were performing. They wanted entertain-ment and I believe we provided it.

Leeds forwards moaned all the time and still take the mickey that I kicked too often on a first tackle. I'd say, "how many times have I done it, scored and we've won games". There would be a muted reply! Roy Francis and Syd Hynes always backed me to make the right decision, even if it did not work out because things came off more often than not. If I had 18 inches to get by my opponent on the touchline, I backed myself. If I got through, I'd cause problems. Coaches offered advice as did my dad but no one actually taught me to play left wing, beat a man or fly-kick on the first tackle. I picked that up, it was instinctive.

Our forwards took some beating. David Ward was Mr. Excitable, especially in a team talk. We used to wind Wardy up in training to get him frustrated and he'd boil over completely. He was a great captain, one of the best skippers I played under and if you lost it he'd have a quick word and it would be "sorry skip" and you'd get on with it. Mick Harrison never took a backward step. He rarely got battered and gave back what he received. In a clash at Workington, Les Gorley hit Mick and left him with a split nose which was a stupid thing to do. Come the second half, Town kicked off and chased the ball. Mick caught it and passed and, all of a sudden, their scrum half shouted, "hey ref, over here." Gorley was absolutely spark out and we all knew why and how.

Our only newcomer to the side was Mick Crane and he was a great buy, a talented footballer with a wonderful pass who was a real character and loved the social side of the sport. His battle with a similar type of loose forward, Harry Pinner, was expected to be one of the key duels. I was opposite Les Jones, like I had been so many times in finals, and he was one of those wingers who I knew I would have my hands full with for the entire 80 minutes.

PLAYING AT WEMBLEY WAS extra special and bizarrely we always had the same dressing room. Waiting in the bowels and hearing the crowd singing 'Abide with Me' was simply spine tingling and the other absolute highlight was walking out of the tunnel end. It was fabulous and I never tired of it. The tunnel sloped slightly from the dressing room so you couldn't see the crowd or they you until you emerged and the whole scene hit you while the noise was absolutely deafening. Lining up, I'd think of all the famous footballers and rugby players that had been there before.

Just as in '72 against them, we got off to a disastrous start. Saints forced Mick Crane to surrender possession and had the first scoring opportunity but Geoff Pimblett was wide with a drop goal. They were soon ahead, though, when Willie Oulton and I failed to take a high kick by Pinner over our try line. The ball went into and out of Willie's hands then bounced into and out of mine and Graham Liptrot touched down. I looked at John Holmes and shook my head but knew it was early in the game.

We were desperate to bounce back. It nearly happened when Sammy Sanderson stole possession from a scrum and almost crossed and Willie missed a penalty when they were caught offside. St Helens were a dangerous team and Sammy was forced to stop Les Jones in his tracks a couple of yards short soon after. Saints kept up the pressure and from a five-yard scrum, Ken Gwilliam sent Bill Francis round behind the posts. Only 13 minutes had gone and we were 10-0 behind when Pimblett converted. A year earlier Widnes would have been tougher to claw back against but Saints allowed you to play rugby, so I thought a chance may come and it did, for me, after around 20 minutes.

Just before scoring, I saw John Holmes take a ball from a scrum and hold it for a fraction of a second and, as a result, one or two Saints players changed their minds from going up into the defensive line towards him. Les Dyl came around the back of Mick Crane and was into his stride. I was ready. The ball came to me 30 yards out and there was no way Pinner or Pimblett would stop me. I got Geoff looking one way over his shoulder and knew that I had him on the outside to score. It was a thrilling effort, made more so when Willie converted from the touchline to get us back into the game.

The lads began to play much better then, although we were still missing tackles and losing possession. Sammy was on song and halted Eddie Cunningham and then it took strong defence to keep out Les Jones again. David Smith went close for us before Saints edged further ahead when Graham Eccles was unfortunate to be penalised for obstructing big Dave Chisnall when he seemed committed to the tackle. Pimblett slotted the goal over and Willie soon had a chance to respond from 40 yards but failed, so we went in at half time seven points adrift.

In the dressing room, there was no panic. Syd reminded us to keep driving forward through the middle and avoid the temptation to move the ball wide just for the sake of it. Yardage was crucial as it would be tight and every point was vital. Our strategy was to come away from Saints' quarter with something whenever we got in there. We had to be disciplined and Syd was sure our fitness would tell in the last quarter. Wardy executed the plan to perfection within minutes of the re-start, surprising St Helens – and the whole stadium – with a drop goal. People wondered why a point at that stage would make a difference but in modern terms, it gave us momentum and we were the ones on the attack. Next, John put in a terrific kick and only a cruel bounce robbed me of a second try. With action at both ends, Saints hit back but we were up to the task, holding Jones and George Nicholls up on our own try line.

Steve Pitchford was more of a marked man after his display against Widnes in '77 but with Mick Harrison and Graham Eccles powering forward, John Holmes looked for options, quickly spotted a gap close in but Phil Cookson was just pulled down short. The move was one in the bank for later, though. We were on a roll and John combined with Neil Hague, onto David Smith, who touched down in the corner. He was going to bring the ball round to make the kick easier but slipped and Willie failed with the difficult conversion. We trailed by just a try and, with 25 minutes left, there was plenty of time to complete our comeback. On the hour, Kevin Dick came on for Sammy who had been a Man of the Match contender but Kevin brought fresh legs. Roy Dickinson then replaced Mick for a final glory charge but Saints were no pushovers and went close to stretching the lead when Pimblett stuck a post with a drop kick. We breathed a huge sigh of relief.

In the last 10 minutes, our forwards at last started to get on top, exactly as Syd had predicted. Steve Pitchford drove forward to gain valuable yards and in quick succession Les and Kevin went close to crossing the white-wash, only for Phil to knock on a clever Holmesy pass close to the line. It was frustrating but we had to keep cool heads. There was still time and despair turned to relief when the two combined again. John fed Phil, who powered over from close range to tie the scores at 12-12. Willie stepped up, although Kevin volunteered to take the tough kick, and was inches wide with the conversion. Nevertheless Saints must have been deflated because they had led for such a long time.

Word came from the bench that eight minutes remained so the next score could be decisive. We felt confident, while they looked nervous. With the game in the balance, there was an announcement that George Nicholls had won the Lance Todd Trophy for man of the match. Back in '68, Don Fox also got the award before the end and ended up with a loser's medal. Maybe history would repeat itself, but we needed something special. With extra-time looming, John Holmes provided it. The lads made a big push forward so the one-pointer was on by the last tackle. John was under intense pressure from a two-man tackle when the ball arrived. He was on his wrong foot but somehow dropped the goal with his left as he was falling backwards. It was a superb effort and took us ahead for the first time with little left on the clock. John used his left foot in training but rarely in a match.

His effort has rightly gone down as arguably the greatest drop goal ever in Leeds RL history.

We looked to seal victory. In the last minute, Phil was stopped yards short and on the next play, Wardy slotted over another drop goal. Ever since, he has said that it was the worst thing he could have done and regrets it because it so nearly cost us the game. Surely, the Challenge Cup was ours but as in '68, there was one final play and one last twist. Saints had possession and got the ball to Peter Glynn who passed to Derek Noonan, seemingly in the clear with the try line barely two strides away. But Noonan, under immense pressure, knocked on. There was much discussion afterwards whether he would have scored but looking back at the replays, he was well covered by our seventh cavalry and close to the touchline. Even if he'd caught the ball, all we had to do was bump him into touch by the corner flag. The lads on that side were absolutely convinced that he wouldn't have crossed. All that remained was a scrum, which we collapsed and managed to see out a few seconds until the final hooter.

After congratulating each other and commiserating with Saints, Wardy lifted the Cup for a second successive year, this time from the Earl of Derby, and we joined an elite group of clubs with back-to-back Wembley victories. I had a third Challenge Cup winner's medal and we were the first side to overturn a 10-0 deficit at Wembley. George Nicholls was officially the star performer but those journalists who'd been forced to choose the award early, when Saints were still in front, must have wished they'd given it to John Holmes for a virtuoso display. He played a part in all three tries and kicked a brilliant drop goal at a crucial time. John deserved the accolade because he had an awesome game, he ruled it at his pace.

PLAYING FOR LEEDS OVER many years was magical. Competition was tough facing the likes of St Helens, the Hull teams, Castleford, Featherstone, Warrington, Wigan and Bradford – pundits couldn't pick the top two from one year to the next. Today, fans can't believe the number of strong sides in my era. In 1967, we lost to Featherstone in a Challenge Cup semi-final who beat Barrow in the final, that wouldn't occur today. Clubs complain at the physical nature of playing twice a week but we were faced with three games in five days over Christmas and it was far more physical.

The sport has to move on and I was very fortunate. The '69 Leeds team was a great Championship side while the '75 outfit could match most opponents. All our triumphs were memorable but the '78 Challenge Cup one was particularly special because of our comeback on the day and it was my last Wembley appearance. Honours were great to win and I claimed many at Leeds but the feeling was even better because of the quality of players on my side and in our opponent's ranks. In 1970, when we sat drinking beer in the dressing room in Sydney having won the Ashes, and I'd scored a couple of tries, I didn't think life could get any better but I went on for twelve more seasons after that having wonderful times. I was privileged to play with and compete against the finest players to grace a rugby field and even when we meet up for reunion's now, nothing can take away from that.

What rugby gave me is that all my best mates are from the two generations of players I was with, they are the closest of friendships and they last forever. One of the things about sport is that if you've got your best mate playing with you, you'll always come out on top, that's what it's all about - and you have to enjoy yourself. We laughed with each other even through adversity, had a few cries together and fought in battles side by side. The Leeds club and Headingley ground are, quite simply, the finest sporting environment and rugby venue in the world and I was fortunate enough to play in all the great stadia. Every time I ran down that ramp to the pitch, it was the proudest moment of my life.

JOHN HOLMES
FULL BACK/CENTRE/STAND OFF 1968–1989

BORN 21 March 1952
SIGNED from Kirkstall Boys Club
LEEDS CAREER 625 appearances, 153 tries, 553 goals
HONOURS Championship 1972, runner-up 1970, 1973; Premiership 1975; Challenge Cup 1977, 1978, runner-up 1971, 1972; Yorkshire Cup 1970, 1972, 1973, 1975, 1976, 1979, 1980; John Player Trophy 1973, 1984; BBC2 Floodlit Trophy 1970; 20 Great Britain appearances, 7 England caps, 8 Yorkshire appearances
LEFT Retired

However you define greatness John Holmes fulfilled every criterion. For those who saw him, and there were masses considering he played for Leeds for an astonishing, double testimonial 21 seasons, watching him cajole, toy and orchestrate his side was an absolute joy. A master in 19 finals, and architect of victory in the majority of them, he served notice of his talent with 23 points on his debut as a 16 year old in a Lazenby Cup match against Hunslet in 1968. In his second full season he kicked 159 goals, but it was his sublime timing and passing ability which truly charmed supporters. He was also one of the bravest around, often the victim of horrendously-timed late challenges. Internationally he played in two World Cup finals and by the time he retired he had pulled on the shirt a record 625 times for his cherished club.

Leeds 18 v Widnes 10

John Player Special Trophy final
Saturday 14 January 1984

Central Park, Wigan
Attendance 9,536

Playing thrilling open rugby that defied the worst winter conditions and then producing a heroic second half defensive effort to snuff out redoubtable cup fighters Widnes, Leeds record their only major success in the eighties

Teams

Ian Wilkinson	1	Mick Burke
Paul Prendiville	2	Stuart Wright
David Creasser	3	Keiron O'Loughlin
Dean Bell	4	Joe Lydon
Andy Smith	5	Ralph Linton
John Holmes	6	Eric Hughes
Kevin Dick	7	Andy Gregory
Keith Rayne	8	Steve O'Neill
David Ward	9	Keith Elwell
Kevin Rayne	10	Kevin Tamati
Gary Moorby	11	Les Gorley
Mark Laurie	12	Fred Whitfield
Terry Webb	13	Mick Adams
Neil Hague	14	John Myler
Kevin Squire	15	Eric Prescott
Holmes, Dick Creasser 5	Tries	Linton, Lydon
	Goals	Burke

Referee: W Thompson (Huddersfield)

ASIDE FROM A COUPLE of Yorkshire Cup wins, which is not to denigrate Rugby's oldest competition, Leeds' continuous run of success which represented their second golden era and began in the late sixties, ended in 1979. Five years on, and with most of the players responsible for that unprecedented run of silverware having moved on, gathering dust was becoming the most prominent commodity in the Headingley trophy cabinet. The common thread to those glorious times, and still the classiest act around was imperious playmaker John Holmes. He was one of only two survivors – the other being David Ward – who had been a part of the club's only other success in this competition, in its second year in 1973, when he had gloriously set up the winning try with an outrageous, one-handed, long pass to free John Atkinson. No defender could have read it because he was the only person in the ground who could see the option.

This, though, was the beginning of a new era especially as the international transfer ban had been lifted, an event which saw Kiwi star Dean Bell and Aussie sensation Mark Laurie both make their debuts in the competition, against Hull K.R. and Swinton respectively.

Here, John Holmes harks back to a filthy afternoon in Wigan when Leeds answered those critics of the game who were becoming concerned that, with players becoming increasingly athletic and six-tackle tactics more predictable, the fare was becoming sterile. Playing thrilling open rugby that defied the worst winter conditions and then producing a heroic second half defensive effort to snuff out redoubtable cup fighters Widnes – with the ceaseless and indefatigable Laurie to the fore on both fronts – blue and amber ribbons were again back in vogue. For a brief moment the Loiners' star was ascendant but this victory represented their only major success in the eighties – and it was some fifteen seasons until the next one came along.

WE WERE PRETTY FORTUNATE to be in the John Player final at all after fluking a win in the first round at Blackpool Borough of all places. They were at the bottom of the Second Division and we were just expected to roll over them but it took a last second, somewhat controversial try to beat them and save the embarrassment of what would possibly have been the worst result in the club's history. I happened to be the one to score it but all the talk at the time was that the winning touchdown came from a forward pass. From what I remember it wasn't, but it was on the margins and for some reason we did struggle that cold afternoon at the seaside. All that mattered in the end was that we got through – we really did it tough again against another Second Division side in the quarter final, at Swinton – but if you make the decider, how you managed it is often forgotten.

That final at Central Park turned out to be my last one for Leeds but I never realised or considered that at the time. I just wanted to play as often and as much as I could and it's like Wembleys, you hope that every time you play there it's not going to be for the last time. I was fortunate enough to go twice on the trot to the Twin Towers in the late Seventies and the same was true with the John Player, we'd been in the final the year before when we'd lost at Elland Road to Wigan. Their winger Brian Juliff scored in the corner and I'm sure there was something wrong with that try, it was either forward or from a knock on, but it counted. Amazingly, it was the first time the two most famous clubs in the game had met in a final.

That was the start of Wigan building their period of total dominance and we were a changing side as well. It had been four years since we had contested a major final and, although we lost in a game that promised more than it delivered, it was good to be back on the big stage. We'd had a bit of a lean period but we never lost the belief in ourselves that we were a decent side because of the players we had. A lot of them had come through and stayed together as a team for a number of years and if we had a blip one season, we were confident we could come back the next because you can't take away the talent.

The John Player run coincided exactly with the arrival of Maurice Bamford as coach for his first spell in charge. I didn't really know him at the time but he was certainly different, I must admit. He had alternate approaches of trying to motivate people, he either built them up or wound them up depending on what they needed. Some he had a go at, others he'd talk quietly to, those were his methods and I always got on with him. He replaced Robin Dewhurst, who I'd known well and for a long time, he was my brother Philip's best man and his playing career at

Headingley was just coming to an end because of a serious knee injury as mine was starting.

Before Maurice had even really had the chance to work with us, we were drawn against Hull K.R. in the second round at Headingley in front of an expectant crowd. They were clear favourites and bang in form while we'd suffered some hammerings at Castleford, home to Hull and especially against the Queensland tourists when we were played off the park. Somehow, though, we got it back together defensively and had a little more strike power with the arrival of Kiwi Dean Bell who scored on his debut as we won a thriller.

Maurice probably did take us back to basics and introduced motivational videos that he had sent over from Frank Stanton in Australia but every coach has his different way and I must have had twelve or thirteen of them in my time there. It had been hard for Robin because he wasn't being given any money to spend on the team but within a couple of years, we were signing a whole side full of overseas players when the international transfer ban was lifted. That first season we got Dean, Steve Martin, Terry Webb and, of course, Mark Laurie and we needed that extra competition for places, they were quality players. When it got out of hand a bit the following season, we were just wondering how many more were going to come as the numbers doubled and then trebled.

Leeds were always on the look-out for players, even while the ban was in force. In that cup winning side in '84 we had Kevin Squire, who was a Devonian who'd come on trial which was pretty unusual. He wasn't around for that long and was a nice kid who I'm glad got to experience winning in that final. He was an out and out tackler but surprised us all one afternoon at Hull K.R.'s old Craven Park when we were getting heavily beaten and he dropped a fantastic goal from near the half way line. I was out that match and was sitting alongside Kevin Dick, who was also injured – there were a few missing that day – and we couldn't stop laughing, despite the score, we couldn't help it. I'm sure when he was asked why he'd done it he admitted he'd forgotten that he was playing League not Union, saying something like, "well it was the last tackle and there was nothing else on." It still makes me smile thinking about it, the whole crowd were stunned.

IN THE JOHN PLAYER FINAL we faced the undoubted cup kings of the time, Widnes, who we'd had a series of knockout battles with in all the major competitions – and especially the Challenge Cup – around that time. We'd beaten them at Wembley in '77 but five years later they stopped us getting back there in the cruellest of fashions, when Mick Adams' kick came back off the crossbar in the final move. It bounced lucky for them and suddenly we were out and devastated. In all the times we faced them, we knew that despite their superb array of talent, if they had one weakness, it was that a number of them were on a short fuse. It was always the same with them, put them under pressure, frustrate them and you knew that, although they were so hard to play against, their discipline would go. It wasn't something we consciously set out to do, we were more concerned with looking after our own game and trying to play football but that was again how it turned out.

I was facing Eric Hughes, a more defensively-minded player used to operating as a speedy centre because Tony Myler, their incredibly gifted creator, was out injured, he never seemed to get a clear run avoiding them. Tony could make things happen but, amazingly, was the only person in the sport that I have never been able to talk to; we never, ever got on. That wasn't the case with anyone else I played against and battled with in the toughest of matches but Tony never spoke. We'd give it to each other on the field, niggling, everything, all sorts went on between us – you couldn't do it now – but we never said a word after the whistle went and I don't know why because he was one of the best stand off halves and footballers that I ever played against. If I met him now I'd tell him that but it was strange.

We beat Widnes the week before the final at Naughton Park in a league game which was a very good result for us, especially as we had a weakened team out – I was one who was missing – but it had no bearing, it never does. What we were developing, though, was some resilience, in virtually all of the previous rounds we'd had to come from behind which was the sign of a good cup fighting team. Again that was down to a belief in the ability of the side. The biggest factor on the afternoon, though, was the conditions. There had been a gale the night before which had taken down half of one of the posts, the wind was still around and there was snow swirling about for most of the game. That affected our approach but we mixed and matched to what we faced and were still determined to play as much running rugby as we could, once we finally got there.

We had terrible travel problems on the motorway getting over to Wigan. The weather was awful which made the journey slow anyway and there was an accident which meant that we only got to Central Park half an hour before the kick off so it was a hasty get changed and straight out for the warm up. It didn't bother me but upset the routine of some. On a normal match day, I'd tend to saunter in no more than an hour before kick off and

David Ward would already be changed and having to be held back. It didn't bother me, I'd get ready ten or fifteen minutes before a game started anyway so I was used to that.

Two of our side were probably in some of the best form of their career at the time. Ian Wilkinson was a terrific attacking full back and we worked well together, with him linking in as I tried to get him on the end of some passes. Defensively, that was where Maurice used to keep having a go, he'd often tell him, "the Queen Mary could turn round quicker" to get him going. He'd had a great season, as had Keith Rayne who'd moved up to prop when we got more second rowers in. I had a lot of respect for him and his twin brother Kevin who were our props in the final, they were good lads who looked after me and Keith was a revelation in the semi-final against Leigh when he scored two match winning tries. That performance and the one in the final probably got him on tour at the end of the season.

The young gun just making his way in the side was David Creasser who'd only come into the team at the beginning of the season and was kicking goals as well. I was helping to look after him a bit out there and it was something of a shame that he kept being compared to Garry Schofield. They grew up together, had been team mates at Hunslet Parkside and came off the same youth tour. Schofield was already making a real name for himself as a try scoring centre at Hull and everyone kept saying about Creas, "is he going to be as good?" Then he had a few injuries that knocked him back a bit but he was very important to us that afternoon.

Maybe because we had arrived late and hadn't fully switched on by the time the match kicked off, we were behind very quickly. Big Mick Burke bust us out wide and sent Ralph Linton over, just as a lot of the Leeds fans who'd been caught up in the jams were coming into the ground at the old dressing room end. We weren't unduly bothered because we didn't feel we'd properly started the game and once we got the chance to move the ball around the way that was natural to us we got into the game, and in spite of the conditions, it paid dividends.

We caught them with two long passes, I used to make the lads run out wide so we could spread the ball, that's the way we trained and liked to play. If the short, direct pass wasn't on, the players knew where to run in spaces and we'd find them. That's how both our tries came about. For the first, Kevin Dick hit Mark Laurie with a long ball. He broke and shipped it on to Belly and I tracked him on the inside for a very enjoyable try. I saw it again a few years later on video and it still looked good. It's always nice to score in a final but, more than that, it was at the time we needed it.

The move worked again soon after, although me and Kev swapped roles. I managed to get Mark away again, he had an absolute blinding game with his constant breaks and tackled magnificently. Everything he did was superb. I think it was the best he played. His coach back home in Australia, the legendary Jack Gibson, who'd recommended Mark to come over to Leeds after winning a Grand Final there with Parramatta, rang the club after the match to congratulate us all which was a nice touch. This time Mark found Keith Rayne and although his pass was slightly behind Kevin, he did brilliantly to take it in one-handed and dive over in one movement.

Just before half time they got back into it with another Mick Adams kick, this time taken by Joe Lydon but I was hobbling out on the wing by then having taken a bang on the leg. There was some doubt as to whether or not I would come out for the second half but Harvey Standeven strapped me up and I was ready to go again. It would have taken more than that to miss the rest of a final. That score just before the break was the end of the tries, partly because the weather took a turn for the worse. It was really bad and we could actually feel the pitch starting to freeze as the temperature continued to drop. It was terrible to play in, I hated it. I played in some games in those types of conditions when you would have been better off putting me in the stand, I wasn't a wet weather player.

What we did have throughout that second half, though, was the spirit and stamina to keep our line intact and we battled it out. We were forced into covering any number of kicks, and we stayed as cool as the weather while Widnes lost theirs. The longer it went on and the more professional we stayed, the more they started going backwards and the inevitable frustration, that we knew was coming, mounted. That was shown in the second half penalty count which was something like nine-nil in our favour, David Creasser adding two more goals as a result, and in the end Steve O'Neill couldn't take any more and got sin binned. Basically their bottle went as we got stuck into them. Our desire was summed up by our skipper David Ward, as ever, who fought on from the front despite a nasty and very painful rib injury. He went off just before the end but nothing was going to stop him picking up the trophy.

David said something afterwards about it being the best Leeds team he'd played in and the papers were full of praise for the open style we'd shown despite the weather. I'm not sure about that. It was a difficult and hard match to play in under those conditions and we had a good team for a lot of years. Mind you, I had to calm Wardy down a lot of times, believe it or not. If anything went mad out there he often needed a quiet reminder.

That win in the final set us on a club record equalling eighteen match unbeaten run so maybe Wardy was right, we can't have been that bad a side. As was so often the case in cup ties between us in those years, though, Widnes got revenge when they beat us in the Challenge Cup semi final at Swinton, with Joe Lydon the star, although Mark Laurie was forced to pull out just before the kick off which affected us.

Back in the dressing room with the little black and gold trophy, the Lord Mayor came in and promised us a civic reception, which we eventually had and was memorable for the inimitable Arthur Clues insisting that we all had a whip round and emptied our pockets for the Mayor's charity. Apparently the final was the councillor's first game of rugby league and he loved it but that hadn't been the end of a difficult yet highly rewarding afternoon. The weather on the motorway was terrible as the snow moved in but the windscreen wipers on the coach wouldn't work, it was unbelievable. We had to follow directly behind the bus carrying the wives in convey, until the usual turning for the 'Wheatsheaf' when the coach seemed to head there almost by itself.

PEOPLE HAVE ASKED ME about my record number of appearances and long service, the way I played and my place in the club's history but I genuinely don't think about it. I was born a bus ride away from the ground in Kirkstall – I used to jump on one to go up to the game whenever I was training or playing – and if I'd had imagined at 16 years-old that I would have enjoyed such a career, I would have kept a diary every day but I just took it for what it was. I can't remember half of it, it just happened and I did it and when people come up and call me things like a legend, I genuinely wonder who they are talking about, it doesn't register. If I've given them pleasure then that'll do me.

It was an almost overwhelming feeling to walk into that first team dressing room in the late sixties as a schoolboy and play alongside guys who only a couple of years before I'd been standing on the terraces cheering as my heroes; the likes of Bev Risman, Atky, Alan Smith, Syd Hynes, Bernard Watson, Shoey, Barry Seabourne, Mick Clark – I could name the lot of them. It was virtually the same team every week – and one of the best the game's ever seen – and within a few months after I'd signed on, I was turning out with them. My dad said that I was as white as a sheet when I first walked out.

I effectively played in three positions, starting at full back, doing a bit at centre and then ending up as a stand off but I was used to that at school.

I was brought up in the centre but played all over so it was nothing new to me. I'd always kicked goals at school as well, banging them in from all over with my eyes closed and I inherited that in the first team. I was told that I could have set a number of records – I got ten in a match for Great Britain which still stands – but I don't know what happened, my confidence went. I captained the side for a couple of years and picked up a Yorkshire Cup but maybe the responsibility did inhibit my play. Wardy took over and we immediately won a couple of Wembley finals, I had no problem with that.

I'm often asked if I have any regrets or if I'm bitter about not being awarded the Lance Todd trophy in the Challenge Cup final in 1978 but people who follow the game and saw that match know what happened. The writers who'd chosen it came into the Leeds dressing room and apologised afterwards because they'd had to vote with ten or so minutes to go when it still looked like Saints would win. They told me I should have got it and that's more than enough. It was by the by, it didn't matter; we'd won the match, that was all that concerned me. It was one of my most memorable wins but we just celebrated with a few drinks afterwards, not a great deal. In the evening we went back to the hotel with all the guests and had a meal with a few speeches. The best time we had was on the Sunday dinner time after everybody else had left. Just the players got together and sat on the floor in the bar and had a beer with each other – that was the most enjoyable part.

I had some terrific times for club and country. I was fortunate enough to be a World Cup winner in 1972 in France as a nineteen year-old and touring down under was one of the best things that you could ever do. I was asked about whether I fancied the chance to play over there but the international transfer ban was on and by the time it was lifted it was probably too late and their interest had waned but I was a Leeds lad anyway. Some of my most rewarding times came at the end of my career when I captained the 'A' team and became a bit of a mentor to the next generation coming through. I played mainly in the back row and absolutely loved it, there was a tremendous satisfaction. It was just great to play among the kids, their enthusiasm and eagerness to learn was uplifting and kept me going for a couple more seasons. Some Thursday nights we'd be playing away in front of only a few people and maybe being tanked and I'd get them together and they'd latch on to a few passes because we'd always try and play some rugby.

I can't really pick a highlight from such a long career and the games that might mean the most to me personally weren't necessarily the big and obvious ones or probably ones that others remember. There was a league match up at Headingley in the mid-seventies against Oldham and we were getting beaten by about fifteen points but I managed to score two tries in the last five minutes and we won the match. Things like that gave me a lot of pleasure. Of course, dropping a goal to win the Cup is a stand out but some of the smaller matches mean as much.

I've been called a reluctant hero. I never really did a lot of interviews in my time – although things were different then and players tended not to make the headlines or be asked as much about the game. Most often after the match it was get a wash, through the gates and go get some dinner at your mam's. If people still mention my name after so long, then that's a thrill.

PAUL MEDLEY
SECOND ROW 1984–1989

BORN   21 September 1966
SIGNED   From Leeds Colts
LEEDS CAREER   102 appearances, 44 tries
HONOURS   Yorkshire Cup 1988, John Player Trophy runner-up 1987/88,
4 Great Britain caps, 2 Great Britain under-21 caps, 3 Great Britain Colts caps,
1 Yorkshire appearance
LEFT   Joined Halifax, January 1989

A local product who played junior rugby with Wyther and Farsley before
signing with the team he had supported as a boy, Paul Medley instantly
became a Headingley favourite. He made his first team debut while still a
teenager and was often used as a game breaker off the bench, his astonishing
pace and powerful surges bringing him a number of spectacular touchdowns
– especially in cup ties. He made a try scoring Great Britain debut in 1987
against Papua New Guinea and, selected for the 1988 Lions tour, he scored
again against the Kumuls in a World Cup-rated Test win in Port Moresby. He
surprisingly joined Halifax, but after just eight games moved on to Bradford,
where he now runs their Scholarship scheme and coaches the Academy.

Leeds 24 v Hull Kingston Rovers 24

Challenge Cup semi-final
Saturday 29 March 1986

Elland Road
Attendance 23,866

One of the greatest cup semi-finals in living memory sees both sides' fans suffer despair, suspense, agony, relief, hope and uncertainty in equal measure, and a young substitute make his name in spectacular fashion

Teams

Ian Wilkinson	1	George Fairbairn
Alan Smith	2	Garry Clark
David Creasser	3	Mike Smith
Tony Currie	4	Gary Prohm
Carl Gibson	5	David Laws
Neil Hague	6	John Dorahy
Cliff Lyons	7	Paul Harkin
Jeff Grayshon	8	Peter Johnston
David Ward	9	David Watkinson
Roy Powell	10	Zook Ema
Kevin Rayne	11	Chris Burton
Terry Webb	12	Phil Hogan
Dave Heron	13	Gavin Miller
Paul Medley	14	Gordon Smith
Keith Rayne	15	Andy Kelly
Creasser, Currie 2, Medley	Tries	Laws 2, Mike Smith 2
Creasser 3	Goals	Dorahy 4
Webb, Lyons	Drop goals	

Referee: Robin Whitfield (Widnes)

LOINERS' 1985/86 CHALLENGE CUP odyssey may have cruelly ended at the penultimate hurdle but they played enough games over a memorable three month period to have lifted the silverware. Normally five wins in the competition would guarantee a civic reception but the Loiners played seven matches in the competition and did not even see Wembley's twin towers. The run started with a Preliminary Round tie on a bitterly cold January night across the Pennines, encompassed two replays and contained a surfeit of magic moments, drama, controversy, determination and excitement to live long in the memory.

The first semi-final clash against Hull Kingston Rovers was described at the time as 'the greatest in living memory' with both sides fans suffering despair, suspense, agony, relief, hope and uncertainty in equal measure. Locked at 24-all, even more excitable supporters turned up five days later to see the resolution despite a foul night – and a second Thursday game in the cup run – to witness another cliff hanger, for the opening forty minutes.

For a youngster just making his name in the sport, playing in front of Leeds' biggest audience, Wembley apart, for 25 years was a daunting prospect and Paul Medley's personal rollercoaster ride throughout the series of games characterised that of the team and the supporters and over twenty years on, the memories still haunt him.

I CAME THROUGH THE early Colts system, which was under 19s and in those days you couldn't sign as a professional until you were 17, which is different to the situation the kids find themselves in these days with scholarships and Academies. Everything was on a part time basis but Leeds had a fine crop, it was quite a rich time for youngsters coming through there.

Just prior to me there had been Dave Creasser, the Mackintosh brothers – who unfortunately never fulfilled their potential because of injuries – Roy Powell and Brendan Hill. That sort of calibre of player had been pushing through, making a name for themselves, including at international level, and we had a large following watching our entertaining games and charting our progress.

I was also pursuing a career in banking which was quite unusual for rugby league players at the time; the more common perception was that they were to be found on building sites or pulled out of the pits and put straight on the pitch but that was changing. We had Andy Mason around then at Leeds and he was an accountant. It was amusing on some mornings at the bank going in with a big black eye and seeing the reaction of the old ladies as they came in to take their savings out. I'm not sure that it was the image the bank wanted to portray.

It was a shock to me to make the Leeds first team so quickly. I got the reputation of being something of a 'super sub', changing games with my explosive running. I signed in July 1984 when I was seventeen and a half and made my debut the following January. In many ways it was a baptism of fire but the game, again, was a different type in those days, especially with the five metre rule, rather than ten, and slower. Consequently, the athleticism and pace I had was more akin to that of a back but I had a forward's build. Nowadays, wide running second rowers are two-a-penny and props have to be athletic as the dynamics have changed but back then I was performing like the modern game is played. Whether I could have survived now, though, is another matter.

I was blessed with a bit of speed and could go the distance so, generally, if I broke through the line I could finish. That was a natural asset rather than a skill but it was great to be able to do it and please the Headingley crowd. Because I was a home grown, Bramley lad who was a teenager playing in the first team and scoring spectacular tries, usually in the corner, they took to me. I didn't really think about the scoring, I just used to run like hell because you had these big guys hounding you up the middle – it was probably more out of fright rather than ability.

Around that time there was an Aussie invasion at Leeds, when the international transfer ban was lifted. There was some resentment from the established lads who saw their places taken but I was thirsting for knowledge. I wanted to push myself as far as I could and learn and develop. Early on I realised that I was fortunate to have some very experienced heads around me like Dave Heron, Kevin Dick, Neil Hague, David Ward and John Holmes – some real stalwarts of the Leeds club. But I also got introduced to some Aussies who had different views and opinions of where the game was and they were the dominant force. They had come over in 1982 – and were to again in '86 – and re-invented the sport and, for me, they had something to offer. It was bizarre to be alongside someone like Wally Fullerton-Smith, who was an international, Trevor Paterson and, later, Peter Tunks and Peter Jackson, who'd played State of Origin and Test matches and I learned a lot from them about how they applied themselves. Mind you, they also taught me some of the pitfalls! To have those guys around and be able to rub shoulders with them was a terrific influence on an aspiring youngster, to see how they prepared and the little things they did, around and within a game. The methodology at Leeds had been to do some training on a Tuesday, do some more on Thursday, a bit on Saturday, then turn up and play. They showed me that there was more to it than that and I got educated about thought and preparation processes away from the club and the game. That was one of the reasons why I later changed my job in the bank to work in a warehouse, of all places, just to give me some more physical activity.

I remember one strange occasion in 1985, around the time I made my debut, when Malcolm Clift had come over in a short term capacity to take over coaching the team after Maurice Bamford had got the Great Britain job and prior to Peter Fox's arrival. I played in one game where I was the only English player on the Leeds team sheet and I couldn't believe it. Our 'A' team that week played Featherstone on a Thursday night and it sticks in my mind that the front row was Roy Dickinson, David Ward and Gary Moorby, while I was stuck in the first team on my Jack Jones. I couldn't understand why I was there playing every week under this Aussie bloke who I didn't know and who didn't know me. I was constantly thinking, 'somebody, somewhere is making this happen and I don't know why'. Roy Powell and Dave Creasser forced their way in and it seemed to be the young lads and all the Aussies. We were trying to suck in their knowledge but occasionally the influx went too far and there was no pathway for domestic players.

Peter Fox came in and was in charge for '86 Challenge Cup run and his appointment was always likely to cause concern among the Leeds fans. They liked the spectacular and the flamboyant and the entertaining, which is probably why they seemed to enjoy what I was doing. They loved the side to side rugby, moving the ball through audacious passes and, often, it didn't matter if there wasn't a try at the end of it or if the side ultimately got beaten. As long as we had a go and the ball was flying all over the place, the errors could be forgiven.

Peter was renowned as a forward driven coach – which is a bit of a misconception because he did have players in his sides with flair – but what he realised was that if you didn't set a platform with your pack, you weren't ever going to be a dominant force and a successful team. Even then, he was an advocate of getting over the gain line, putting the opposition on the back foot and getting a roll on, no matter how much quality you had on the outside. I played with Eric Grothe at Headingley before Peter came in, a massive talent in all senses, but the quality of service he got was so limited. Often it was a case of throwing him a long pass and saying "right, then, let's see what you can do". Nothing was created for him to latch on to. His tries were rarely on the back of opportunities being constructed for him which made his displays all the more remarkable.

A lot of the fans turned against Peter because he was trying to change that around and they couldn't understand a lot of the signings he was making. Gary Price from Featherstone wasn't a wide runner who scored lots of spectacular tries, he was just a consummate professional who did the work. My defence wasn't the best at the time but the old adage applied to me, as far as the fans were concerned, it didn't matter if I let in four tries as long as I scored five. That was why, over the years, Roy Powell and I complimented each other so well. I got all the glory but he did far more for me than anyone else. He just grafted, took the ball forward and basically allowed me not to do the tough stuff but wait to take advantage of it on the outside.

WE'D NOT HAD A great season in 1986, with the low point being knocked out of the John Player Trophy at Second Division Barrow – that's when the knives really started coming out for Peter. I only played about twenty minutes in that game. I took a whack to the head that needed six stitches and I was in cloud cuckoo land. I didn't really get the sense of the Challenge Cup being our last chance saloon, being young I was just loving playing first team rugby in front of fantastic crowds and scoring some great tries. Life couldn't have been much better for me whether we were losing or not. Leeds fans always have been fickle, I remember once – after winning six games in a row – we got booed off after Warrington absolutely hammered us and Mark Forster ran four tries round me at left centre. I was having a ball, though, and at 19 years of age I wasn't concerned with what was happening to the coach or how the team was going. I was merely fighting like mad each week to keep my place and just doing whatever I was told. Even though the fans seemed to love me, the only bloke I had to impress was the one who was picking the team – as I later found out in 1989.

Once the Cup came round, we had to play a preliminary round tie at Swinton on a miserable Thursday night and it was made worse for me because I chipped a bone in my wrist. An easy win qualified us for a trip to Halifax to face the eventual league champions and no-one gave us a chance there, especially because the pitch was frozen solid and the atmosphere, as well as the conditions, incredibly hostile. I was still out recuperating and I listened to the game on the radio as Tony Currie tore them apart.

I also missed lowly Doncaster giving us a fright at home, after the game was switched from their Tattersfield ground, but was back for the epic quarter-final against Widnes. They were the undoubted cup kings at the time and, again, few fancied us travelling to Naughton Park and surviving. I nearly scored straight from the kick-off, I went down the touchline side and Mick Burke just got across to bump me into touch by the corner flag. I did get over twice early on and although David Creasser missed both conversions, he kicked a last minute penalty from the side line right in front of the bench to secure a 10-all draw. I did my shoulder scoring one of the touchdowns and that was the start of my on-going problems with the joint which I took on tour but shouldn't have done.

I played in the replay against Widnes but was nowhere near fit and that was an incredibly tough encounter won on kicks as we triumphed 5-0. I struggled through it in a lot of pain and discomfort. There wasn't the kind of injury management that there is now and, in hindsight, I shouldn't have played but I was so desperate because there was a semi-final on the horizon.

The draw was no kinder to us as we faced the defending champions Hull Kingston Rovers, who were a dominant force at the time. We all thought that if we could beat them, in what would be another massive clash, we would be in prime position to go on and win the trophy. We'd proved we could defend against a great side like Widnes with the Hulmes and Mylers in their ranks and we knew that if we could maintain that and play a little as well then we had a great opportunity, especially as the game was on our doorstep at Elland Road and we would have terrific support behind us. I can't recall ever having a bad game at that stadium. It's always been a great platform for me and a ground that I've really loved playing at, I don't know why.

We started really well, Dave Creasser slipped through a gap to score in the corner and then Tony Currie crossed, from a brilliant switch by Jeff Grayshon, while being tripped by Paul Harkin. Harkin had to go, although there was lot of discussion at the time about whether it should have been a penalty try and the kick awarded in front of the posts, especially as Dave – crucially as it turned out – hit the post with the conversion. Despite that, those of us on the bench were thinking, 'it's all going great'.

We were ten points up and with a man advantage and one of their hardest forwards, Chris Burton, had gone off after breaking his arm on Kevin Rayne's head. I don't think that consciously we eased off, after all we landed two drop goals to keep the scoreboard ticking over, but the twelve men dug in and got back into the match thanks to a very controversial try. David Laws quite clearly dropped the ball as he went over in the corner but unbelievably it was given. Suddenly, the mood on the bench changed to 'it isn't going to happen, it's one of those days' and there was a feeling of foreboding as nothing seemed to be going right and the match was turned on its head.

It got worse, somehow Hull KR established a ten point lead with the two Smiths superb and we found ourslevs scrapping to stay in the competition. Time was slipping away and I wasn't even out there. I was sitting in the dugout saying, "I want to get on, I need to get on" and feeling totally useless. I'd never played in a semi-final before, the ultimate Wembley goal was passing us by and having watched those huge finals as a kid all my life and been in the crowd cheering at them, all I wanted to do was be involved to help try and get us there. I didn't have the command to go up to the coach and say, "come on, it's my time" because the response from Peter would undoubtedly have been, "kid, sit down, shut up, tha' knows nowt". I just had to bide my time and hope for an opportunity but also at the back of my mind was the thought that because it was such a gripping game – one of the best semi-finals ever seen – that I might not get my chance because you wouldn't want to throw an inexperienced youngster into such a cauldron.

At the other end of the age and experience scale, Jeff Grayshon set up a try for Tony Currie that got us back into the contest. In his long and distinguished career, Jeff had lost in numerous semi-finals and this seemed to be his last and best chance of finally stepping out at the Twin Towers. He was within a whisker of it but the whole squad was desperate to get there.

I was finally allowed on and, almost immediately, Cliff Lyons picked up a loose ball and in a flash threw me a peach of a pass. I was straight into a gap and facing one of the best and strongest defensive centres in the world, Kiwi international Gary Prohm. Maybe he underestimated this fresh-faced lad in front of him but I just handed him off, went round him and was gone. I was fortunate to have the pace and strength that belied my stick-like look and before he could re-adjust, I was over the line. What I'll never forget is the Leeds fans' roar when they realised we were back in the driving seat, it nearly rocked the foundations. At 24-all, we'd rescued the game and looked set to claim it only for Dave Creasser's relatively easy conversion to drift wide of the posts. I was certain we could still win it but panic set in and we had David Ward trying to drop goals on the second tackle. Despite his knowledge and vast experience, that just showed what the carrot of Wembley can do to players who knew better. He was trying to do the right thing, take everyone by surprise and was only 25 metres out but it flapped and missed. It was nip and tuck and both sides knew that any mistake and you were gone, that was it.

When the whistle went and it was still all square, it was the oddest feeling and strangest atmosphere. We'd expended all that effort but we hadn't won or lost. Some of the more experienced guys sensed that, being against twelve men, our opportunity had passed. There was also the added factor that both sides had to play again the very next day in a league fixture, so you had to think about preparation for that and, indeed, I played most of our home game against Bradford. There was also frantic work immediately going on behind the scenes to ensure that Tony Currie and Cliff Lyons, who had been due to fly straight back home to start their club season over in Oz, could hang around for the replay.

THE 33,000 WHO TURNED up, back at Elland Road, on the following Thursday night was the biggest crowd I'd played in front of. The Saturday attendance had been unbelievable, especially as the drama unfolded before them but the noise at the next one, under lights, was phenomenal. The place was full and the atmosphere was spine tingling. That was especially so for me because this time I was in the starting line up, swapping with Terry Webb, rather than having to wait until late on to get my chance. Perhaps Peter thought that I was unpredictable enough to offer more of a threat and, although the scoreless first half was a real war of attrition, I did

Lewis Jones (top row, far right) presides over his men during the epic 1957 Cup run. Also pictured are Don Robinson (top row, second left) who, along with his exceptional skipper, became the first Loiners to hold cup and championship winner's medals, and Lance Todd trophy winner in the final, Jeff Stevenson (bottom row, second left)

Seemingly unflappable, elegant, quiet, intense and a wonderful sportsman, Lewis Jones (right) carved an everlasting niche in Loiners folklore in helping Leeds defeat Barrow in the 1957 Challenge Cup final.

Colin Evans spots a gap by the posts to make it 8-0 despite the best efforts of Harry Major. Lewis Jones raises his arm in acclaim in the background as referee Ronnie Gelder awards the try.

Derek Hallas goes airborne over Joe Pickavance to post his first of two sensational touchdowns in a glorious five minute spell that defined his Leeds career – from this moment Leeds fans knew that the 'holy grail' was within touching distance.

One of the greatest Leeds sides in the club's history prepares for the journey
to Wembley with Tony Crosby (top row, second left) next to try scorer in
the final John Atkinson (top row, far left). Bev Risman's (bottom row, far
left) goals proved crucial but it was the one missed by Don Fox that wrote
all the headlines as the silverware came to Headingley.

Forever known as 'Watersplash' Wembley, the heavens opening
in the lead up to and during the game leading to farce, furore
and fervency in equal measure.

Effervescent scrum half Barry Seabourne watches anxiously as
Ray Batten typically gets the ball away despite the sub aqua conditions.
In the background, Bill Ramsey and Mick Shoebottom crane their necks
to follow the play.

'It's Ours' – the Leeds players revel in their unexpected moment as the
sun finally comes back out. Mick Clark, displaying the coveted Challenge
Cup, is hoisted by Alan Smith holding the lid as a crouching John
Atkinson claims the base.

Ready for battle as skipper Barry Seabourne (front row, middle) takes his men into the fray at the cavernous Odsal bowl to face fierce rivals Cas. John Atkinson's (top row, second right) sensational last gasp try and Bev Risman's (bottom row, far left) nerveless goal brought Leeds the title for the second time.

The Lord Mayor of Leeds fetes the Championship winners on the Civic Hall steps in the middle of one of the most glorious eras in the club's history.

One of the youngest front rows ever selected for a final take on and master the might of St Helens; Roy Dickinson (back row, fourth left), Steve Pitchford (back row, middle) and David Ward (back row, fourth right) never made a backward step, fully justifying the faith of legendary coach Roy Francis.

Leeds, despite being underdogs, take the first ever Premiership trophy. Syd Hynes shows the silverware with two-try hero Mel Mason (front row with scarf) enjoying his finest hour.

(Top row, left to right) Alan Smith, John Atkinson, Phil Cookson, Stan Fearnley, Mick Harrison, Steve Pitchford, Roy Dickinson (Middle row, left to right) Paul Fletcher, David Smith, Graham Eccles, David Ward, Les Dyl, Brian Murrell, John Homes (Front row) Neil Hague, Kevin Dick.

Desperately saddened by death of Chris Sanderson at Salford in the lead up to the Final; Leeds collected the Challenge Cup in his memory.

The 'bionic barrel' on a roll, Steve Pitchford charges away from the
Widnes cover on one of his trademark barnstorming runs that won him
the Lance Todd trophy.

Inspirational skipper David Ward, grasping the silverware, is chaired by
Neil Hague with grinning teenager Kevin Dick alongside him revelling in
his first ever cup tie – his cheeky dummy for the crucial try the defining
moment as the 'cup kings' were downed.

Phil Cookson's close in plunge past Eddie Cunningham and Harry Pinner draws the side's level with barely five minutes to go. John Holmes, who – as ever – supplied the perfect pass, reels away in delight. His sensational drop goal then completed the miraculous recovery.

John Atkinson doing what he does best, skinning defences with his blistering pace before planting the ball in the corner for another classic winger's try on the big occasion as the Leeds fans go wild.

David Ward's (front row, with ball) men, orchestrated by veteran John Holmes (top row, far right) turn disaster into glory on an 18 match unbeaten run that took in the John Player Special Trophy. It was 15 years before major silverware was back on the Headingley sideboard.

Kevin Dick somehow gathers a pass that was behind him with one hand while evading the Widnes cover for a glorious try in the most difficult of conditions.

Kevin Rayne makes ground with Cliff Lyons in support on the inside in the first of two enthralling semi-final ties at Elland Road, which drew over 55,000 fans in total.

Ian Wilkinson is prevented from getting the ball away as Leeds stage a late comeback to draw the initial tie. Their resolve was finally broken in the second half of the replay.

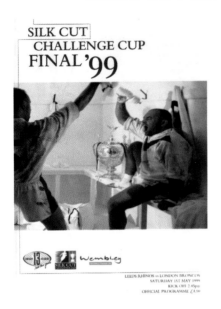

Leroy Rivett creates history by becoming the first player to score four tries in a Challenge Cup final on the day Rugby League said goodbye to the famous Twin Towers.

The young Leeds flyer gets outside Dean Calloway and makes it into the corner as London Bronco's spirit is finally quashed and the Rhinos rack up a record score.

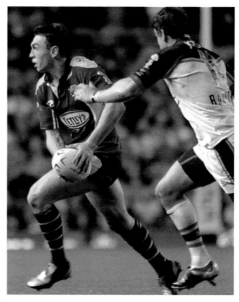

A sell out Old Trafford Super League decider sees Kevin Sinfield lead his men to the ultimate glory with a masterful performance by hand and foot. Here he evades Bradford back rower Lee Radford's challenge.

One of the longest sporting waits is over, as 32 years of hurt is banished. Kevin Sinfield lifts the Super League trophy as Ryan Bailey and Rob Burrow begin the beer shampooing.

With a characteristic skip and dart, Danny McGuire looks to break the Canterbury Bulldogs' line in front of a packed Elland Road crowd that revelled in the Rhinos' glorious first half display.

Skipper Kevin Sinfield and ace try scorer Danny McGuire show off the trophy which signifies that Leeds are the best club side in the world.

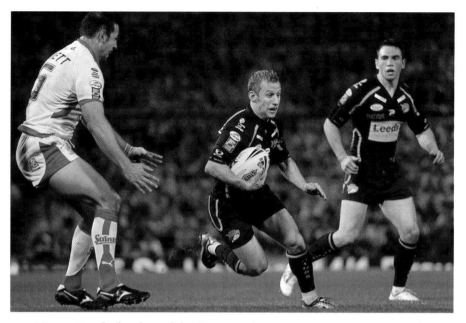

Harry Sunderland Medal winner Rob Burrow scampers past Mike
Bennett with Kevin Sinfield in support. The 'pocket rocket' was
a sensation as St Helens were rocked on their heels.

Clinton Toopi (right) and bearded Jamie Jones-Buchanan cheer on
Lee Smith as he comes down with the ball after outjumping
Francis Meli for the crucial try.

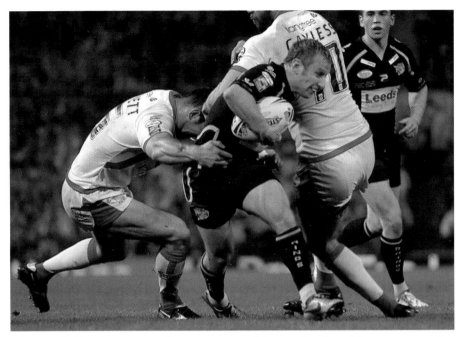

They seek him here . . . Mike Bennett and Jason Cayless fail to get to grips with Rob Burrow as he again torments the Saints midfield with another energy-sapping, zipping burst to put his side on the front foot.

Leeds fans at Old Trafford count down the clock and acclaim arguably the finest performance ever in a final by a side wearing blue and amber.

make one of the few clean breaks only for George Fairburn to cut down my options. I was deep in my own half when I saw space and broke clear and, as usual, just put my foot down but all credit to George, he lined me up, forced me to try and take him on round the outside and he absolutely leathered me. I knew I'd been hit big time but that was his renowned calling card. I managed to just get up and play the ball but I was groggy and he let me know in no uncertain terms that if I came through again, "I'll be waiting for you, son". It was quite a shock, like I'd just run straight into a wall. To hit me as hard as he did in open field left me in awe of his talents. I'd been able to go round a lot of players when I was in full flow but he was the first full back to really smash me and it left a physical and mental impression.

It was actually a much tighter, more nailbiting game than the final 17-0 score line indicates and, as opposed to the eight glorious tries a few days before, chances proved to be very limited which is why George's intervention was so important.

At half-time, with us tied at 0-0 at that stage, it was becoming increasingly apparent that the first score was likely to be the crucial one, although the game on the Saturday had proved that both sides had the capability to strike back when behind and seemingly out of it. In the dressing room the mood was 'nothing gained, nothing lost' but the talk alluded back to the Widnes replay and that it was going to take something special to break either defence down. That was why when the first try did come, it was so disappointing. Aussie prop Peter Johnston just burrowed through us from about three metres out. It was such a soft effort in a game like that, it was criminal. Paul Harkin – who because the disciplinary hadn't had time to sit, wasn't banned – had already got them on the board with a drop goal realising how important such a deadlock-breaking score was but we were still in the game, especially when we were awarded a kickable penalty which would have taken it back to a converted score difference. Unfortunately, David Creasser missed it and our chance had gone. We didn't have a recognised goal kicker at the time, someone like Frano Botica who came along a few years later at Wigan, kicked goals for fun from anywhere and forced people to realise the full importance of a quality goal kicker and the difference that made in tough, tight games. If we'd landed that penalty, I'm sure it would have given us just the lift we needed to feel we were genuinely back in the match. There's a huge pressure on kickers but if it had gone over in a game as intensely emotional as that, with our energy levels visibly declining from the effort we were expending, it would have been just the boost we needed.

At times in matches like that you are physically out of it and you need something psychologically to raise you out of the mire. Two points would have made us forget how tired we were and what we stood on the verge of losing and given us the belief to go on and do the job. As it was, Hull KR got the benefit of the relief of the miss and it gave them a second wind. They scored two late tries to inflate their victory margin. After their first of those I'd been substituted and so I had to watch the final drama, and the ultimate gut-wrenching disapointment, unfold in utter dejection from the bench.

FOR A NINETEEN YEAR-OLD, those two matches in such a short space of time, in front of over 50,000 people in total, were experiences I'll never forget and that still, to this day, leave a bitter taste that makes me shiver at the recollection. I had the whole of my career in front of me but I sat in the dressing room afterwards and saw two of the toughest, hardest blokes I have ever played with – David Ward and Jeff Grayshon – in tears. Jeff, at 37 years-old, knew it was his last chance gone and it was as close as he'd ever been, effectively 40 minutes away from Wembley, after a career of over 15 years. His dream was shattered. I had the rest of my rugby life to get there – even though, as it turned out it actually took another ten years – but I witnessed this absolute warhorse realise that his opportunity had gone and I felt guilty that I hadn't done something out of the ordinary to get him there. I was mortified and I didn't feel that I had done enough for these two blokes I so admired and who had busted a gut to the wall. It brought it home to me how brutal the game was off the field as well as on it and the emotion they played with in those games was unbelievable.

We had two massively draining games in the space of six days what with the crowd, the atmosphere, the build up and expectation before the second encounter. The first had been so good that it made a nationwide impact, it had been a massive spectacle that was immediately labelled one of the best ever seen and the same was anticipated again for the replay – it even got extra television coverage on the BBC that night. That's why the crowd went up by half again, fans just wanted to be there. Afterwards, we were all at such low ebb, it was almost like a death within the family. The next training session we went to was desolate; there was no enthusiasm, nothing.

LEROY RIVETT
RIGHT-WING 1995–2000

BORN 17 December 1976
SIGNED From East Leeds ARLFC
LEEDS CAREER 58 appearances, 30 tries
HONOURS Grand Final runner-up 1998; Challenge Cup 1999, runner-up 2000
LEFT Joined Huddersfield Giants, 2000

Leroy Rivett created history on a red-hot day at Wembley in 1999 when he became the first player to score four tries in a Challenge Cup final – one, a 90-metre interception, winning the BBC's Try of the Season. It was a glorious feat that won him the Lance Todd trophy. That, though, was his career peak and, with a change of coach for 2000 at Headingley, he found himself out of favour. Re-called for the first Challenge Cup final to be hosted at Murrayfield, he turned from unknown hero to scapegoat villain, dropping two early high balls from Henry Paul to concede tries from which the Rhinos never really recovered. That was his last appearance in blue and amber as he embarked on a nomadic career, the victim of unexpected fame and a host of niggling injuries.

Leeds Rhinos 52 v London Broncos 16

Challenge Cup final
Saturday 1 May 1999

Wembley Stadium
Attendance 73,242

Fun in the sun in the capital as Rivett runs riot in the last Cup final under the Twin Towers

Teams

Iestyn Harris (captain)	1	1	Tulsen Tollett
Leroy Rivett	22	2	Rob Smyth
Richie Blackmore	3	4	Greg Fleming
Brad Godden	4	22	John Timu
Francis Cummins	5	5	Martin Offiah
Daryl Powell	13	6	Karle Hammond
Ryan Sheridan	7	7	Shaun Edwards (captain)
Barrie McDermott	10	12	Steele Retchless
Terry Newton	21	26	Robbie Beazley
Darren Fleary	15	27	Matt Salter
Adrian Morley	11	11	Shane Millard
Anthony Farrell	17	23	Robbie Simpson
Marc Glanville	12	9	Peter Gill
Marcus St Hilaire	14	13	Mat Toshack
Lee Jackson	9	15	Dean Callaway
Andy Hay	16	3	Chris Ryan
Jamie Mathiou	20	17	Glen Air

Rivett 4, Godden, McDermott St Hilaire, Harris, Cummins	Tries	Offiah, Simpson, Fleming
Harris 8	Goals	Smyth 2

Referee: Russell Smith (Castleford)

RECORDS TUMBLED AS LEEDS, in their first Challenge Cup win in 21 years and roared on by an estimated near 50,000 bedecked fans, said goodbye to the Twin Towers in the last decider before Wembley's re-development to end a decade-long trophy drought. Their route to London, to play the side that represented the city, could not have been tougher, facing the three other so-called blue riband sides along the way and being underdogs each time.

Whether or not a £12,000 a man win or nothing bonus helped steel their resolve, they overcame a sending off to defeat Wigan, showed great patience to dispose of St Helens and came from ten points down to defeat fierce rivals Bradford in the semi-final. Becoming the massive favourites in the decider, Leeds took an hour to fully find their feet against a game Broncos outfit before turning in an exhibition performance to capture a host of records.

In the heart of it was a young, unknown, happy-go-lucky winger Leroy Rivett, who recalls that glorious run and his magic moments when the nation stopped and marvelled at his finishing ability, first seen against Wigan in the third round as he showed a clean pair of heels to put 12-man Leeds on the road to glory. His meteoric rise peaked at the Twin Towers barely two months later, but, it seems, he has no regrets or misgivings about the way things worked out.

LEEDS' VICTORY IN THE 1999 Challenge Cup final against the Broncos is a day I will never forget. The club hadn't won the trophy for twenty one years but approaching the final, for me, winning it was not some sort of 'Holy Grail' quest. We knew our supporters were desperate for success but I wasn't hung up on hoodoos or superstitions, it was just the biggest day of my career and something to look forward to rather than carry any extra baggage into it. Previous defeats in semi-finals and finals were part of the club's history and although a lot of the guys had been involved in them, everyone was determined that it would not affect our approach to that game, especially after the road to getting there had been such a tough one.

One of the odd things about the game was the overwhelming number of Leeds fans, wishing us luck, seeing them travel down and in the stadium. Normally the split is half and half come Cup final day but we outnumbered the London fans and neutrals by about six to one. Our only focus was not to let them down and to make their day out in the sun the best it could be.

Scoring four tries took time to sink in, I was on cloud nine with the achievement but that was only part of it. As a young boy, I'd supported Leeds, so everything about the occasion and its outcome was magnified. Fans naturally think that those touchdowns are likely to be the most out-standing moments but for me a lasting memory I will always savour was walking out of the Wembley tunnel. That's the goal of every player. To achieve it, aged 22, and having watched so many finals on the television, was fantastic.

We lined up in the tunnel and waited for what seemed an eternity. I just wanted to get out there. First, you need a signal from the BBC, which seemed to take forever, and then it comes. You can hear the Wembley roar, it's electrifying and you can almost taste it. You start walking up the slope and the tunnel entrance gets bigger. In the dressing room beforehand, coach Graham Murray had said, "stay together, be a team. Don't be overawed by the occasion, don't be looking for people in the crowd. Keep your focus and think about the job in hand". But then you walk out and it is unbelievable. Nothing can prepare you when it's your first game at Wembley. The hair stands up on your arms, the atmosphere is buzzing, the roar thrilling. There was just a mass of people and you can't help but try and spot family and friends in the crowd. It was enormous and enchanting. That fuels your determination to succeed.

AS A SPORTSMAN, YOU shouldn't need someone to motivate you to be your best. If you do then you're in the wrong game. I'm a competitive person, an all-rounder. I liked racket sports, football, pool but rugby league was my main passion. I grew up in Leeds and started out at Pendas Panthers before moving to East Leeds, who had a great tradition in amateur circles in the city. I played on the wing in a strong team. We won a number of trophies, including being the first club to win the BARLA National Youth League and Cup double in 1995. Scouts were watching and I got invited to train at Headingley, although I was reluctant at first because I thought the set up might be too big for me. Castleford were interested but a group of us went down together to Leeds for trials and I was one of a handful of hopefuls to be signed up.

As a kid, Ellery Hanley was my hero. There were not many top black players in the game at that time and I aspired to be like him. I loved watching the Challenge Cup finals on television when Wigan dominated from the mid-eighties. They had great players like Shaun Edwards, Andy Gregory, Martin Offiah and Ellery. He was skipper at the Loiners when I joined, which was a thrill and a reason for signing but I never played a game alongside him as it turned out. I put pen to paper in 1995 and made my debut a year later at St Helens, in the first season of Super League. We played back to back campaigns because of the switch to summer and that was a drain on all the clubs' resources, especially as it turned out at Leeds.

It was a hot day at Knowsley Road. We got beaten heavily and I didn't receive many running chances. At the time, I wasn't ready for such a physical challenge and felt intimidated and a little bit unsure.

I was in good form during the 1997 season, as the club was bought out and became the Rhinos, and I scored plenty of tries for both the Academy and Alliance sides. First team opportunities were limited but I did get to go on tour for the World Club Challenge. All the Super League outfits faced their NRL counterparts and we were in a pool with North Queensland and Adelaide. Leeds coach Dean Bell took me as a fringe player. It was a fantastic experience and I played against the Rams on the famous Adelaide Oval.

During the following year I was loaned to neighbours Bramley to keep up my match fitness, Leeds had some feeder link up with them at the time, and then finally started to get established in the first team. We made the play-offs and probably our best performance came in the final eliminator as we thrashed Saints at Headingley to qualify for the first Grand Final against Wigan. I scored a hotly contested try at the start of that game. It was a debatable one and the video referee took an eternity but gave it and that got us on the front foot. We played some terrific stuff after that. Old Trafford was a thrill, the crowd was excellent even though the event wasn't as established as it is now, although the rain stopped us playing our natural flowing game. Jason Robinson scored a fantastic try that proved to be the difference and despite battling away, it was not to be. The defeat hurt but it also gave us a taste of the big time which stood us in great stead come Wembley in '99.

Pre-season training was tough but I felt an integral part of the squad and my game was improving as a result. By now I was also used to our preparation for games. The early part of a week concentrated on rehab and video work, analysing our own performance, weights and field sessions. A number of the lads also did extra sprint training early in a morning, working on our speed and technique with Texan conditioner Edgar Curtis. He was great for me and I missed that specialist work when I left Leeds. Towards the end of a week, it would be lighter sessions and on a match day we'd be in 90 minutes before kick-off to make sure everyone was on board with Graham's game plan.

In those days, the Cup occupied the early weeks of the season so you could really focus on it as a separate challenge. We couldn't have been given a much more difficult opening round when we were drawn at home to Champions Wigan, who were desperate to wipe out the memory of their shock defeat to Sheffield at Wembley the previous year. Our task wasn't made any easier when, early on, and holding a narrow lead, Barrie McDermott was sent off for a high shot on Simon Haughton. That called for a real back to the wall effort but, as often happens, the twelve men pulled together in adversity. I managed to score before half-time to keep us ahead and in the second forty we played superbly to hold on and record a stunning win in front of the television cameras.

All of a sudden we were installed as favourites but the next round gave us as tough a hurdle to overcome when Ellery's St Helens arrived at Headingley. There was some turmoil in their camp, he was new there as coach, was marking out his territory and refused to do an interview for the BBC before the game, but that siege mentality in their dressing room made them very difficult opponents. Fortunately we were at home and the crowd helped will us through after we'd gone behind early on. Ryan Sheridan poached a crucial score just before half-time, they – surprisingly for an Ellery side – lost their discipline and gave away a number of penalties as their frustrations mounted and we held on. Having beaten two of the other top four sides, there was a real buzz inside our camp that it just could be our year. With the squad more or less the same, carrying the recent bitter memory of defeat in our previous final also spurred us on.

We did the expected job at Widnes in the quarters, running away with the game in the second half. I managed another try and youngster Kevin Sinfield made his mark after looking a fantastic prospect in the Academy.

WE DREW BRADFORD IN the semi-finals. They'd beaten us at the same stage the previous two years and a lot of people in the game, including some of our fans, felt that we'd bottle it again against them. The Bulls had such a huge pack which we'd struggled to cope with in the past, but we sorted them out this time round. As the big boys had been drawn together, it meant an unfancied side, either Cas or London, was set to make Wembley. No-one really said it but in a way, our semi looked like it would determine the eventual winners.

I always liked playing at Huddersfield's McAlpine Stadium – as it was then known. We prepared well and felt good but before we could settle we were ten points down and then they had a try disallowed for a forward pass which, in all honesty, would probably have been too much to come back from. It took a stroke of individual genius to get us back into it, Ryan Sheridan disappearing from behind a scrum to rip the ball out of Danny Peacock's hands and race away for a try that surprised the whole ground and the television cameras. I was jogging back into position to defend and then all of a sudden the Bulls players were protesting and the referee was going to the video screen. When we saw what had happened, it gave us a massive boost and seemed to deflate them. If ever there was a game breaking moment, that was it. Ryan was sensational during that cup run and so was Iestyn Harris who crossed for the winning try five minutes from the end. We just went berserk, we knew they couldn't come back and the Wembley dream was a reality. I'll never forget the feeling of pure elation on the final whistle and the celebrations in the dressing room afterwards.

I'd been to Wembley as a spectator in 1988 to watch Wigan beat Halifax and now my chance beckoned but Graham Murray left us in no doubt that we had to play for our Final places. I missed the comfortable Easter win in the dress rehearsal against London Broncos at Headingley when Paul Sterling came back into the side but returned and scored twice in wins over Hull Sharks and Huddersfield. It was a strange time. The Giants game was one when you didn't want to get injured or make a mistake but still play well enough to impress the coach for the following week. I must have done okay because soon after it Muzza confirmed I'd be starting and it just meant everything, I was overjoyed.

There was a togetherness in the side, more so than in any other team I played for during my career. There were plenty of jokers with Terry Newton at the centre of dressing room banter. Graham had numerous qualities but he was best at breaking down barriers. There were a number of 'unknown' players in our squad, like me, Marcus St Hilaire, Brad Godden and Darren Fleary but we had instilled into us a desire to play for each other. We were not household names like, say, Jason Robinson, Paul Newlove or Henry Paul at other clubs but Graham was big on activities to develop team spirit. He instilled rules so the squad got to know each other and played as a unit.

Our match preparation for the final, training wise, was as near to a normal week as possible before we travelled down on the Thursday. Of course, there was a lot of media hype and attention and the fans came out in force to Headingley to wish us luck as we set off. We then trained at Eton College where disaster so nearly struck. I rolled my ankle in the final session. The only thing in my mind was that I was so close to achieving a life goal that I dare not tell anybody. For a while there was the horrific realisation that I could be out of the final but the staff applied ice, I took it steady for the rest of the day and night and fortunately things worked out okay.

I slept well and during the night woke up for a drink after dreaming that I'd scored a hat-trick in the final. The thought made me smile but I didn't tell the rest of the lads at breakfast for fear of them taking the mickey out of me even more then they normally did. What I did feel, though, after that was that it was destined to be our day.

We then had a muscle-loosening walk and a team meeting before the short journey to Wembley. Sitting on the coach, I looked round and had huge confidence in my team-mates. Skipper Iestyn Harris was making a real name and reputation at the time, he had a cool head on young shoulders, great vision and was a massive influence on the side. Often he came up with a special play to get us out of trouble or on a roll and the tactic of keeping him out of the way of the opposition forwards at full back early on, before moving him up to stand off to destroy them was a masterstroke. He always seemed to have time on the ball, was a superb kicker, which tended to maximize our threat, and was composed – an ideal quality at the back which spread through the team.

Inside me, Richie Blackmore was a man mountain, the perfect winger's centre. For a big man, his skill level was awesome and quite often I had no idea how he'd managed to get the ball away to me in space. Opponents had a fear factor about him, they were wary of his power and his touch and never knew whether to come in and cover him, if they could, or stand off him and risk him bursting through. We got on really well on and off the field, it's fair to say that he looked after me. Brad Godden and Franny Cummins had a similar partnership on the left.

Our half-back combination, for me, had the edge over London pair Karle Hammond and Shaun Edwards. Stand off Daryl Powell was the ultimate professional, competitive and aggressive – someone who always performed to the best of their ability. Ryan Sheridan was the ideal partner, quick off his feet and with his wits, combining a terrific side step and a real terrier-like attitude.

Up front, Barrie McDermott was someone you'd hate to play against. An animal on the field, he was a gentlemen off it and a great example to the younger players. He worked hard at his game, clearly loved being around the place, led the camaraderie in the dressing room and was always going on about the 'Oldham mafia'. He frequently let us know how skilful he was and not just a season ticket holder at the disciplinary hearings! Fellow prop Darren Fleary was in a similar mould, although quieter. He knew his limitations, had a basic game plan but just went about his business incredibly efficiently. He was also one of the genuinely hardest men in the game. When he hit you in the tackle, you felt it. He and Anthony Farrell were inseparable. Along with Marcus St Hilaire, they were the 'Huddersfield posse'.

We had the best of both worlds at hooker – Terry Newton and Lee Jackson – even though both the guys would have liked more game time. I'd played with Terry in the Academy and he'd started out in the back row but once he switched to the engine room, he never looked back. Terry went on at the start to absorb and give out the strong arm stuff and then Lee came on with his speed out of dummy half to terrorise tiring markers. Tez and Adrian Morley came over together from Lancashire and Moz was just about reaching his prime. A magnificent athlete with a lethal tackle, like Barrie, he was someone opponents would think twice about running at. Although nearing the end of his career, Marc Glanville was immensely appreciated by his team-mates. He was the one who was always tidying up for us even though his knees were shot. He was brave, strong and a massive influence on the pack. If we needed impact off the bench, then Andy Hay was the ideal man to bring on.

Like many people, I was surprised London Broncos had reached the final. I'd watched their semi against Castleford at Headingley the day before our game with Bradford and what a match it turned out to be. In a way, I'd rather have played the Tigers in the final because of the derby element. The rivalry was intense from their side in particular. They just loved beating Leeds and it would have spiced up the decider. Virgin boss Richard Branson was behind London Broncos, so there seemed even more coverage in the media than usual. Reporters picked up on every angle imaginable, even the fact that my sister worked for Virgin as a flight attendant, so had a foot in both camps. London had a number of good players, especially Shaun Edwards and Martin Offiah, who'd made their names at Wigan. Although at the end of their careers, both were dangerous and potential match winners. Martin still had tremendous acceleration and big-time experience. You couldn't take him lightly if you were opposite him, even though he had lost a yard of pace.

We knew that if we looked after our own game, then everything else would take care of itself. I was buzzed up, I thrived on the crowd, when I ran out the roar always inspired me. It was tough playing in front of a few hundred for Bramley but a Challenge Cup final at Wembley was the stage I lived for.

REPORTERS SAID WE MADE A rocky start when Martin Offiah scored on five minutes but I wasn't worried. We had confidence, our form was good, we were favourites and we would prove why. We had plenty of experienced guys who urged us to keep our composure. Then London shook us again, Robbie Simpson took a Hammond pass in his stride, making it 10-0 in as many minutes. Leeds supporters must have thought, 'oh no, here we go again, always the bridesmaid,' but I was still feeling okay. We just needed to get going.

Iestyn got our first points with a simple penalty following a high tackle by Shaun Edwards on Ryan, then I scored my opening try. Daryl Powell made the break and found me with a looping pass on the wing, just out of Offiah's reach. I stepped inside and out past John Timu before touching down and it felt fantastic. I loved scoring and to do it on that stage with the huge Leeds contingent screaming me all the way was just something else.

It was nip and tuck right up to half-time with London probably shading it. Sometimes you get moments which are pivotal to the course of a game and Ryan's cover defence to stop Hammond when it seemed he must go over between the posts changed the match. That was a huge part of his game and one that was undervalued – but not by his grateful team-mates.

Then, right on half-time, Brad Godden combined with Lee Jackson to score our second try. It was a strange one, though, as Brad spun out of a tackle, passed, received the ball back and fell over the line between the posts. Iestyn converted and suddenly we had the edge. I walked off feeling fortunate because London had been in the ascendancy for much of the half but came off with little to show for their efforts. Graham Murray reinforced the things he'd instilled into us that we needed to do but felt we hadn't put into practice and we came out determined to kick on.

Credit to London, they began the second half well, put us under the cosh and it paid off when Greg Fleming scored a third try, which Rob Smyth converted. We had to react and did with a try after Simpson was harshly penalised for a late tackle on me. Barrie blasted through four London players to touch down and has lived off that score ever since. He refers to it as "the winning try" and, to be fair, it probably was. Iestyn converted to put us in front again and suddenly we got on a roll. Ryan Sheridan put in a 60-metre break, Iestyn switched play to Anthony Farrell onto Ritchie Blackmore who offloaded to me and I was over for my second try in the corner.

London now had to score twice and they gave it one last shot but we knew that another score for us would all but settle the match. Marcus St Hilaire provided it on the hour as London tired. Credit to the Broncos, they continued to press but their hearts were broken when I read a ball from Hammond who was under pressure and tried to find Tulsen Tollett with a wide ball. I stepped in, pinched it and was away down the wing, never expecting to score. On television, my third and most memorable try may have looked straightforward but my legs were going to jelly. The try line never seemed to get any closer despite the crowd being up and roaring me on. I didn't look over my shoulder and negative thoughts just went through my head. My legs felt heavy like lead and I was saying to myself, "don't fall, don't trip". I was sure I was stumbling but on the replay I wasn't and there was no-one near me. It was bizarre, there was no thought that this was my hat-trick try, I just felt I couldn't make it.

When I touched down, I was shocked and overwhelmed. For a winger a long distance try is always special but at Wembley even more so and I knew we'd definitely won because of it. One of the lads mentioned I'd be getting £10,000 for grabbing a treble but I didn't absorb that until later.

The pressure had gone. We had daylight and relaxed while London crumbled. Iestyn and Franny went over, then I got my fourth try in the last minute to create my own piece of history, though I didn't realise it at the time. I was 35 metres out when Richie gave me the ball with little space. There was work to do but I fended off two opponents before dancing down the touchline. There was no thought of how many tries I'd scored, it was a matter of doing what I loved best.

At the final whistle we were euphoric and then all you want to do is look for friends and family. We climbed the stairs of the Royal Box, Iestyn collected the famous old trophy, we all lifted it in turn and Graham Murray carried it down. On the lap of honour, we enjoyed the moment in front of the massed blue and amber fans and then there was complete pandemonium in the dressing room. To set personal and team records in the last of the finals at the old Wembley and before its demolition added to our triumph.

Unfortunately, I was unable to enjoy the celebration meal or homecoming on the open-topped bus because I had bad stomach cramps. Maybe it was down to the excitement. It was surreal when my dream of scoring a hat-trick came out in the media after the game. I couldn't get enough of people clapping me on the back. I thought I was level-headed but it was hard not to become wrapped up in it all.

AFTER WEMBLEY, WITH A new higher profile, things changed for me. Suddenly I was marked tighter and it made things difficult. Twelve months on from my greatest moment, the press slaughtered me after the Challenge Cup final against Bradford at Murrayfield. I was unable to get near a couple of high balls, which Bradford scored from but I wasn't the first person to make such a mistake and won't be the last. Reporters were harsh because overall I didn't feel as though I played that badly, I just made two bad mistakes that were so noticeable. As a winger, if you score you're the hero but if you make a mistake chances are the opposition will. I experienced both extremes of a Cup final.

I didn't play for Leeds Rhinos again. I'd been out of favour in 2000 with coach Dean Lance which really disappointed me. We'd made a terrible start to the season but got through to the final to defend our silverware and there was a feeling that I was a big match player so faced Bradford, but it didn't work out.

I wanted to put things right but never got the opportunity. I went on to play for a catalogue of clubs without ever really settling; Huddersfield, Keighley, Warrington, Bramley, Doncaster, Chorley, Leigh, a spell in union with Otley, Villefranche and Hull KR. Critics said I partied too much and fell out of love with the game but I simply didn't have that hunger after leaving the team I dreamed of playing for as a kid.

Some people don't understand that sentiment but I'm a passionate person and can only do things I believe in otherwise it can be a struggle to get motivated. I'm still passionate about rugby league and try to get kids involved. I've taken some with behavioural problems that I work with at Leeds Junior YIPS (Youth Inclusion Projects) to Headingley. I love that type of work. It's somewhere you can take youngsters and they feel safe. Rugby league is a family sport, fans integrate; they sing, chant, it's a great experience.

I enjoy reflecting on the '99 final because the memories return. It's always there and doesn't take much to bring it all flooding back. Richie Blackmore was carrying a knock so gave me a lot more ball than I'd usually get. A lot of my success that day was down to Ritchie not being quite right, just offloading and letting me have a run. Every Leeds player performed on the day and Ryan Sheridan was a strong contender for the Lance Todd Trophy before I scored the third and fourth tries. Ryan had a fantastic game because he was a playmaker and try saver at crucial times.

For me you could not have written a better script. I wasn't sure I'd be in the senior side but then got in, nearly had a last minute injury and then I had to borrow a pair of Iestyn's boots for the final. I had studs but it was a hot day, the pitch was hard so I needed moulded treads and Iestyn had a spare pair. I wore his 'magic' dancing boots. Maybe I should have worn them a bit more! I wish I'd have kept the boots and got them framed.

There is disappointment that I did not kick on and make more of my career but on the flip side I achieved more than many players and enjoyed my time in rugby league, both in terms of the places it took me to and people that I was privileged to meet along the way. Some legends of the game never experienced winning the Challenge Cup at Wembley. I feel honoured to have achieved what I did and it's terrific to be associated with a final when records were created. They are made to be broken but I hope my four tries in the Challenge Cup final remains forever. At the time, I'd never scored a hat-trick for Leeds, so my haul made it even more special.

I experienced both ends of the spectrum in the finals I played in. They say that sweetness is never as sweet without the bitter, and the heartache against the Bulls certainly makes the victory against London taste that much better.

KEVIN SINFIELD
LOOSE FORWARD/STAND-OFF 1997–PRESENT

BORN   12 September 1980

SIGNED   From Waterhead ARLFC and made his way through the Academy ranks

LEEDS CAREER (to end of 2007 season)   271 appearances, 53 tries, 740 goals, 15 drop goals

HONOURS   Grand Final 2004, 2007, runner-up 2005; World Club Challenge 2005; Challenge Cup runner-up 2003, 2005; 14 Great Britain caps, 4 England caps, 4 Lancashire appearances

Kevin Sinfield is the only Leeds skipper to lift two Championships, in 2004 – after a 32 year wait – and again at Old Trafford in 2007. He was also the first to see his men crowned World Club Champions. Earmarked as a leader from his early days skippering successful Academy sides; his perception, dedication and intellect mark him out as one of the professional era's finest exponents. As well as showing immense composure and supreme oratory skills during Super League XII, he also became the first Leeds player in history – and second in Super League – to play and score in every match during a season, a total of 36 games and 306 points. By the end of 2007 he had become the club's third highest points scorer and was granted a testimonial.

Leeds Rhinos 16 v Bradford Bulls 8

Super League Grand final
Saturday 16 October 2004

Old Trafford
Attendance 65,537

Leeds claim their first title in 32 years in front of a capacity crowd

Teams

Richard Mathers	21	6	Michael Withers
Mark Calderwood	18	17	Stuart Reardon
Chev Walker	5	16	Paul Johnson
Keith Senior	4	4	Shontayne Hape
Marcus Bai	22	5	Lesley Vainikolo
Kevin Sinfield	13	18	Iestyn Harris
Danny McGuire	6	7	Paul Deacon
Danny Ward	19	8	Joe Vagana
Matt Diskin	9	1	Robbie Paul
Ryan Bailey	8	29	Stuart Fielden
Chris McKenna	3	12	Jamie Peacock
Ali Lauitiiti	29	13	Logan Swann
David Furner	11	11	Lee Radford
Willie Poching	16	10	Paul Anderson
Barrie McDermott	10	15	Karl Pratt
Rob Burrow	7	27	Rob Parker
Jamie Jones-Buchanan	20	19	Jamie Langley
Diskin, McGuire	Tries		Vainikolo, Hape
Sinfield 4	Goals		

Referee: Steve Ganson

LEEDS RHINOS, UNDER NEW coach Tony Smith, were in irresistible form during 2004, losing only two and drawing two of their 28 regular season fixtures. Finishing nine points clear of their nearest rivals and scoring over 1,000 points – with Danny McGuire registering 39 tries – they entered the championship play-offs in prime form. Losing to arch rivals Bradford in the opening round, they fought back to beat Wigan at Headingley before claiming their first title for 32 years against the Bulls at a packed Old Trafford. At the heart of their long awaited and immensely cherished victory was outstanding skipper Kevin Sinfield, who during the campaign had landed 152 goals – the sixth best return in the club's history – totalling 323 points.

Here he divulges what that victory, after a generation of disappointment, meant to everyone at the club. He outlines his relationship with and the impact and philosophy of Tony Smith, now the Great Britain and England coach and Performance Director at the RFL. He recalls the unique Friday night atmosphere at Headingley Carnegie stadium and the personalities within the camp, one of whom nearly missed the Grand Final after suffering an injury in the warm up. He also explains why a midweek trip to a deserted Old Trafford was a key factor in ultimate victory and how, like in 2007, proving people wrong was a huge motivating force.

THE RHINOS SQUAD GOING INTO 2004 was settled. I'd just signed a new five year deal at the club which indicated how happy I was to continue learning at Headingley Carnegie. I'd been there for nine years at the time, having joined in 1994 as a thirteen year-old, and was given my first team chance quite early in my career. By the back end of 2003 I was captain of what I consider to be the greatest and a really special club. Other than being my birth place, it felt like home; especially in terms of the many good, life long friends I've made there. Leeds, as had been talked about for many years, was a sleeping giant and I hoped and believed that my future and theirs would involve some silverware.

What came into the mix was Tony Smith. I didn't know him at all, my first dealings with him were in 2001 when went on a pre-season trip to Jacksonville together with Huddersfield and he was their coach. We played against them in a twenty minute hit out at the end of the tour and I actually scored two tries and had a decent game and when he arrived as Leeds coach I was hoping he would remember that. When we first met, he was really refreshing, honest and smart technically. Within just five minutes of talking to him, I knew that he was going to bring an edge to us and we were all going to learn; in some ways, it was like stepping back into school. That season we gained so much individually and collectively and Tony was the instigator and catalyst.

He pretty much said straight away that I'd be retaining the captaincy. We'd lost some experienced players in 2002 – the likes of, Andy Hay, Ryan Sheridan, Karl Pratt, Iestyn Harris – and Tony recognised the need for stability. He was really supportive of me, it was a nice time to be at the club and the first pre-season sticks in my mind. Among all the usual hard work and graft, there was a lot of intelligence in there that instilled a confidence in us which, come the Grand Final, stood us in good stead.

The side was relatively young, and although defence was key – Brian McDermott took control of the majority of that and did a fantastic job – the accent was on flair and expressing ourselves. That changed the axis a little from previous Super League campaigns when the onus of the successful clubs had been on pure power. The mix between Brian and Tony was outstanding, they got on really well and discussed things deeply and in depth and even disagreed from time to time, which I've always believed is healthy.

In attack what Tony brought in was that everyone had to move on every play and be there next to their team-mate instead of the ethos that it was your carry and then see how we go. That support mentality spread throughout the team on both attack and defence and when you've got guys around you who are prepared to cover your backside, then you've got the basis of a winning team. Tony also broke all the skills down in an effort to go back to and stress the basics, we were doing the kind of drills that you would expect an under nine's team to practice. At the time it seemed a bit mundane and demeaning but it worked, standing still on a freezing field at Kirkstall passing a ball three metres, three hundred times. It wasn't the most entertaining but we all bought into the principle, understood the reasons why and within a matter of days, you could see the benefits. Skill was a big factor for us that year and that sort of training was the foundation.

However much it hurt, getting knocked out of the Challenge Cup early aided our Grand Final ambitions and that's one of a number of parallels that can be drawn with our 2007 success. We then got a good hiding at Saints and the video session after that sticks out; it was then that we saw the ruthlessness in Tony's nature. He shocked a few people in the room but we used the subsequent weeks off we got when others were playing in the Cup to hurt a bit more, train a little harder and get our knees dirty. We turned the disappointment to our advantage. We had to put all our eggs in one basket and were incredibly focussed on winning at Old Trafford. There was a huge amount of hunger about the place with some eager young lads balanced by more senior guys who had not won titles and there was a massive determination to change things.

We had huge expectations ourselves but we also knew exactly what the title meant to the fans and those combined forces continued to drive everybody week after week which showed in the consistency of our performances. We were never satisfied, we wanted to continually improve and that was what our priority became rather than what was on the scoreboard. That was another change of emphasis; instead of worrying about needing to win, we concentrated on performing well in the knowledge that on the back of that, results would come and they did.

The atmosphere changed within and around Headingley Carnegie Stadium. We started getting more sell out crowds which generated an even greater, special spark and that fed the momentum. The supporters were fantastic and it had probably been a long time since the famous old ground had rocked like it did in 2004. To look round, we had everything we wanted; sunny, summer Friday night games, the place was full of young families and fans who'd watched the club for sixty odd years all dancing and enjoying the entertainment and it was a really good place to play. You could sense, even walking out for the warm up, how much everybody was behind us.

Leading the side out, because of the support we had, was not just extraordinary but also touching.

If that combined enthusiasm was embodied within anyone, it was Richie Mathers; he was like that every day. He loved training, playing, being integral to the team and had been a massive Leeds fan all his life. He played a huge part in the celebrations after every try we scored and that sort of natural exuberance breeds within a squad. His form generally, having broken into the side, was outstanding and he played a big part in what we achieved that year.

There were no additions to the ranks at the start of the season but part way through Ali Lauitiiti joined and that was another massive boost – when you see him with that big smile, you know everything is alright. In his first game, at Bradford, he was outstanding. There had been a few clubs in for him and the Bulls were one of them. I remember sitting on the bus after the match thinking, 'I'm glad he's on my team'. His skills were second to none. What he could do with the ball was amazing and he was at his best when he was constantly frightening defenders by running at them, no matter how many were round him.

As a finisher, Danny McGuire is up there with the best there has ever been at the club and when he was sniffing, a lot of others gave up supporting – if there was a try to be had, he'd be grabbing it. He scored some crucial ones in his superb tally and always seemed to be coming up with the goods when we needed it.

In his final season, David Furner was tremendous and we became great friends during his time at Leeds and still speak regularly now. He'd been and done it in both hemispheres and at the time I thought he was a great signing and so it proved. He supported me in any and every way he could; for a young captain he was one of the vital older heads that I needed around. We hit it off really well almost straight away and the manner with which he conducted and looked after himself at training, the family man, the way he played, everything about him was an eye opener to the rest of us. He did a fantastic job and his influence should never be underestimated or forgotten. He probably should not have played in the Grand Final, he got injured in the warm up, but he never let it show, played a vital role and it was a fitting way for him to finish. Being there for him at the end of his career meant such a lot and for someone who'd done everything in the sport to be so emotional about playing in that match showed just how much he'd bought into being at Leeds and how much he meant to the guys.

WE FINISHED THE REGULAR season with the League Leader's Shield and with it came even greater expectation and hype after such a long time since the club were last champions, but that three week period coming into and including the play-offs was my favourite time. Despite the build up, there was still a sense that there wasn't that much confidence in us and Bradford beating us fairly convincingly at home in the Qualifying Semi-final was probably the best thing that could have happened. We talked about it being the kick up the backside we needed but from that moment on, things couldn't have gone any better as we developed a siege mentality. Even some of our most passionate supporters in many ways doubted whether we could win the title and maybe some of the players did too. But after the Monday video session following the Bulls game, it was do-or-die again and by the middle of the week we were ready for whatever it would take to win the competition. It's my favourite memory because it's nice to prove others wrong for writing us off. The guys showed a lot of character to come through that and what Leeds is all about.

We'd played Wigan at the same stage and venue the year before and got beaten but by the time we faced them in the 2004, we were just dying to get back out there, show what we could do and put things right. Thankfully we did that and whatever the Warriors tried to throw at us, we were going to be bigger and better than them – there are direct similarities with the equivalent match against them in 2007 – and after the first ten minutes, when we were sensational, we knew that if we continued to play like that, we could win the Grand Final. Victory also re-fired the fans who shared in the joyous celebrations of qualifying for Old Trafford.

That extra tie meant that we had only a week to prepare for the ultimate decider. I think you say that you'd rather play that extra game if you go on and win the Grand Final, if you lose then you claim that you needed the week off. It's a tough one but because of the confidence the Wigan win gave us, we were ready, we were bouncing and the guys were excited. They just wanted to get out there again straight away. If we'd had to wait a fortnight some of that impetus could have drained away. Grand Final week is always a busy one. There are a lot of media duties to undertake, people mithering you left, right and centre for tickets and a whole variety of things to do and take care of that are different to a normal game, so it probably suited us to go immediately into all that. The on-field build up was pretty low key; we had quite a light week in training and no matter how Bradford were intending to play, we were sure we could handle it. We had a lot of reasons for wanting to win but had learned quickly from what had happened the fortnight before against the Bulls and we were totally determined to ensure that their physical dominance over us was not going to re-occur.

My first introduction to the 'Theatre of Dreams' was at the formal media day on the Monday before the game and I was pretty much in awe of the surroundings. We were not used to that whole build up and, when you get to have the usual captain's picture at the side of the trophy, it hits home how big a sporting and life event it is going to be. Not just for yourself but also for family, friends, supporters and everyone who was a part of the club. That's a terrific, inspiring feeling but you also get excited about running out on to that tremendous arena with its superb surface and even though it was empty, I wanted to be in the middle and to play there and then.

We went back to Old Trafford as a team on the Thursday and I have some really good memories of that day. The authorities there actually let us out on to the pitch, which apparently is never normally allowed to happen there, and everyone had their phones out taking pictures. We had a bit of a get together in the middle of the field and you could see at that moment from the look in the lad's eyes that they understood the true significance of the occasion and that they were going to be totally focussed come kick-off time. That visit definitely helped with our visualisation and calmed a lot of nerves about what to expect while exciting the boys even more. We were able to realise that it was just another stadium, a piece of grass and that we had a job to do on it. If we'd have turned up on game day and had our first look then, with the crowd already in, it might have been too much for us. It was vital to familiarise ourselves with the environment beforehand and we were ready.

TONY HAD MADE CHANGES TO the side every week during the regular season but come the Grand Final he named the same team as against Wigan the week before, which shocked a few in the media and also meant that Matt Adamson, in particular, missed out. That's where a coach earns his money. It's a real tough part of the job and it also causes mixed emotions among those who are selected. If you're in the team, you are obviously incredibly elated about the opportunity but the flipside of that is some of your mates are unhappy but that's one of the toughest elements about sport, unfortunately. Not everyone can win, some don't even get the opportunity to perform and it was extremely hard for a guy like Matt. He'd played for something like eleven seasons in the NRL, was at the end of his third year at Leeds and seemed destined never to play in a Grand Final. It was also tough on Andrew Dunemann and the likes of Francis

Cummins, who'd been a club legend, and Wayne McDonald. They were guys at the back end of their careers; it wasn't as though they were young-sters just starting out who you could console by saying that there would be another chance for them. If we'd gone on and lost then people would have undoubtedly criticised Tony for his selection choices, which always happens, but thankfully we got it right. I do feel for those guys who missed out, they played as much a part in that year as anyone who did run out in Manchester and fully deserved their winners' ring. I know myself from getting a Challenge Cup winners' medal in 1999 that it doesn't actually mean as much if you're not out there battling on the day. That's not to say I'm ungrateful, it's just that it doesn't have the same resonance if you don't take part in the contest when the trophy is lifted, any player will tell you that. I really felt for those who missed out but it certainly didn't stop them enjoying the eventual celebrations.

There wasn't really a big captain's speech in the dressing room before we went out because things just felt right and the occasion didn't warrant it. You could tell from watching everyone prepare that they were ready and just wanted to get out and nothing I was likely to say was going to change the way that they were planning to play. It was about setting out to enjoy ourselves, that was our stage and we had the opportunity to show the world what we could do individually and, more importantly, collectively; to make a stand and show that we were not chokers.

Waiting to run out on the lush turf was a little weird. You are in the tunnel for no more than a minute or so while the television gets ready but it feels more like three hours. You can hear everything but you can't see outside and it is all a bit gladiatorial. You are expectantly waiting to enter the arena to go out and do battle and then suddenly the doors open, the light shines right through and you can see the illuminated trophy, the soldiers guarding it and then the fireworks go off all of which makes the hairs immediately stand up on the back of your neck. The walk out is a really special moment but for me it is about totally focussing at that point because otherwise you can get really caught up in it. I try to enjoy the run out for the warm up, take everything in then, usually fill up and get rid of the raw emotion in that instant. Come the match, it's just nice to be able to sprint out, because you're excited, you break off, there are no anthems and away you go which is good. To see the blue and amber everywhere was incredibly special, though.

I don't know whether the grass had been watered, but it was very dewy underfoot and that also accounted for the way the game was played. We'd gained a reputation for fast, expansive rugby and scored over a thousand points during the season but in big games it's often about doing the basics well and not making mistakes that matters most. We knew that they would throw everything at us early on and we would have to weather their storm. They were the bigger side but we felt our fitness would tell and it could be the last minute when we snatched victory, so we had to stay in the contest, which meant eliminating errors.

Later in the game we opened up and got our reward but early on it was important to calm any nerves and build a foundation and we did that. The other key tactic was to target Lesley Vainikolo but for that to work Mark Calderwood had to be on the top of his game. For me, that year, he was the best winger in the competition and a close second was Marcus Bai. The combination of the two was formidable and they were both tremendous finishers. Marcus was like having Barrie McDermott out wide but with pace and fitness and Calders was also a natural flyer. All year, whenever we kicked to the right hand touch line, he harassed his opposite number, either tackling them just as they got to the ball or running straight past them to score a try. We knew he could do that all game and in the Grand Final he had Les in his pocket.

For me, kicking at goal is especially important in the biggest games because you know that you are not going to get that many opportunities. The chance to put over an early penalty was significant. Not only was it a settler for the side but it was a nice moment to know that all the practice I'd done throughout the year was still with me on the biggest night. That was also a change in tactics, all year we'd tended to run penalty awards – and been criticised a number of times for doing it – but on that occasion, going for goal was the right thing to do.

We then went behind when Lesley crossed for a try but that didn't dent us. We knew how good a side they were and one full of great attacking players, so nilling them was always unlikely. We anticipated they would tire in the closing stages of each half and that happened, so there were no self doubts when the 'Volcano' put them ahead. It is only natural to raise questions about your worthiness in the lead up to a huge occasion, especially when wearing such famous colours and all they confer. You don't want to let your team-mates or the city down but, once you're out there, it's about your next action when you've suffered a temporary set back.

We had to make certain that our response was a positive one and it was. It came from Matt Diskin with his sensational try and he was pretty excited after he'd got it having burst past two outstanding Great Britain players to score. He was another who'd had an absolutely outstanding year; he was fit, lean, quick and a huge threat. His touchdown was a special moment for him and the rest of us as you could see by the way we all rushed over to jump on him in celebration. If there had been any lingering concerns, that try and the manner of it got rid of them.

Bradford had a touchdown disallowed when Lee Radford passed after being grounded and Shontayne Hape went in but huge occasions usually contain big decisions and the debate that's prompted is what sport is all about; without it, nobody would be interested in going and watching. Fans will always have opinions and argue about outcomes but if you take that out of the mix then rugby league wouldn't be the addiction it is when it grabs hold of you. The human factor is a vital part of it and I don't think the officials made an error in that case.

Just before the break I got the chance to put over another penalty to give us a six point lead and to have any sort of an advantage at the break was important. Bradford were the masters at winning Grand Finals and for us to go in with a significant buffer and the confidence that went with it was crucial, which was why it was right to take the two points on offer again. It was an incredibly fast and physical game and in those types of encounters, it is imperative to get your scores whenever you can.

WE KNEW THEY'D COME out strongly at the start of the second half and despite Tony stressing during the interval the need for discipline and not conceding points first, we gave away two cheap penalties in succession which set the position for Shontayne to go over for a try near the corner. Perhaps crucially, Paul Deacon missed the difficult conversion from out wide, which meant we were still in front. That showed the importance of goal kicking, which was something I was acutely aware of, not necessarily even for what it does for your own side but the lift a miss can give to the opposition. We didn't have to change anything, if Bradford were prevented from scoring again we'd win and we still felt in command. We took one on the chin and got on with it.

There was nothing between the sides for the next twenty five minutes, Bradford made one clean break – which could have been a match winning one – but Chev Walker got back to snuff Lesley out. Chev was another of the predominantly local, Academy-produced core of the team that was at the heart of its spirit, which is something the club prides itself on. His tackle was probably a defining moment. When big Les breaks into the clear, it's hard enough to haul him in but to give him a head start and then come from nowhere to chop him down was a truly special effort from Chev and he put in a massive performance that evening. It was one of a number of times throughout the contest which proved that no matter what was thrown at us, we were going to pull together and someone would clean up.

After those heroics, Marcus's sensational forty metre kick return set up the position for the clinching score. When you've got a winger built like him and as quick and determined as he was, then we had our own 'volcano' in many ways. Everyone had a key role to play in the victory. From that break, Robbie Paul subsequently knocked on and that gave us the attacking field position to really screw some nails in to their coffin and build some pressure as their big men began to look fatigued. It gave us the chance to camp down in their quarter but it only took one more play to effectively seal the game.

Danny McGuire started and finished the move but Keith Senior's role in sensationally off loading to get the ball back to him shouldn't be over-looked. Keith was another who was almost impossible to stop when he found some room but who was often unfairly criticised for his handling even though he is a great provider. Danny, as only he can, was instinctively back on his shoulder and dived over at the Leeds end to huge jubilation from us, led by Richie of course, and the fans that had waited so long to savour such a moment. I still had to kick the goal but as soon as it went over, everybody knew we'd won. At the end, the significance of bringing the title back to the club after such a long wait was secondary to finding the nearest person to hug. For me, that was Chev and he was crying; it had been an incredibly emotional journey for him, in particular.

Before I could put my hands on the trophy and open the champagne, I had to make a speech to the crowd – which included family, friends, people you go to work with every day – and a watching, live television audience. Even though it was a daunting task, the adrenalin had already kicked in. Thinking back about it still scares me now but you could have asked me to undertake anything at the time and I would have done it. I was proud to be in that position; it was an honour and a truly special moment because a few seconds later I was going to lift a trophy that meant so much too so many. Some people who had played a big part in the success needed to be openly thanked and, at the time, in terms of public speaking, it was actually one of the easiest things I have had to do.

The stadium authorities wouldn't let children on the field for the lap of honour but we all climbed over to where our wives, partners, families and kids were and that was another incredibly emotional moment. We've got pictures at home of myself and Jayne with Jack, who was barely three weeks old, fast asleep.

Everyone asks you what you are going to do with your Grand Final winner's ring and everything up until that point had gone to my mum and dad but that was the one thing I wanted to give to Jack straight away and that's why the winning of it meant everything to me. They're not an expensive item but in terms of the intrinsic value it has, the way it was won and it being his first game, the significance was awesome. The stewards didn't have a clue what was going on but it was a wonderful interlude for me, particularly as we were being thrown hats and scarves and you could just see how overwhelmed everyone was.

After we'd got changed and on the bus to make our way back to the Long Bar at Headingley Carnegie, all the lads were singing – some went on to have a wild night – and just to have ten minutes to let the impact and momentousness of what we'd achieved sink in, was truly amazing. It was probably the first moment in my life where I had some real satisfaction from rugby and sport. Obviously you win trophies as a kid and enjoy it but to be somewhere you've wanted to be since you were eight or nine years old was magnificent and momentous. To quietly drink that thought in while the guys were going crazy around me was immense. It was something that I wanted to recapture and that point was stressed in the lead up to our latest success.

BECOMING THE FIRST LEEDS player to play and score in every game in 2007 is really hard to appreciate when you're still involved. I'm a goal kicker anyway, I practice to land them and I don't like missing games. I was fortunate to stay injury free that season and when you talk about it in those sorts of terms; you should be doing it every year. Nevertheless, if it was so easy I wouldn't have been the first to achieve it. I'm sure in years to come I'll realise the magnitude of it. Playing for Leeds is an honour and when you get to make history and leave a legacy, you can't ask for more, although I don't think about landmarks like that at all, if I'm honest. The team winning and being successful is what drives and motivates me. I do feel extremely lucky to have captained the club to two titles, especially because there are so many great leaders within it and a lot of people have supported me throughout. I'm incredibly fortunate to be the one who gets to pick the trophies up on their behalf at the end of it, have the pictures done and be the centre of attention for a few minutes but it means a lot more to me than that. I do understand that one person needs to be the figurehead but I do feel humbled that it's me.

DANNY McGUIRE
STAND-OFF 2001–PRESENT

BORN 6 December 1982

SIGNED From East Leeds ARLFC and made his way through the Academy ranks

LEEDS CAREER (to end of 2007) 158 appearances, 129 tries, 2 drop goals

HONOURS Grand Final 2004, 2007, runner-up 2005; World Club Challenge 2005; Challenge Cup runner-up 2005; 12 Great Britain caps, 1 'Northern Union' cap, 4 England 'A' caps, 1 England under 21's cap

Some players have the look of something extra special about them the minute you see them. Even in the Rhinos' Academy ranks, stand off Danny McGuire looked the real deal; his pace and instinctive, natural awareness bringing him a hatful of tries and marking him out as one of the most outstanding emerging talents. In 2004 he set a joint Super League record of 39 touchdowns as Leeds took the title, scoring the winner in the Grand Final and being voted the 'Rugby League Writers' Association Player of the Year'. His poaching ability in the Leeds number six shirt inevitably led to comparisons with Garry Schofield and, although maintaining his near try-a-game ratio, he had developed into a complete play making pivot by the time Leeds again carried off the domestic crown in 2007, becoming one of only seven Rhinos to own two winner's rings.

Leeds Rhinos 39 v Canterbury Bulldogs 32

World Club Challenge
Friday 4 February 2005

Elland Road
Attendance 37,028

Leeds become the best side on the planet with McGuire having a hand in four tries and scoring one himself in a first half of pure, stunning rugby

Teams

Richard Mathers	1	1	Luke Patten
Mark Calderwood	2	2	Hazem El Masri
Chev Walker	3	3	Jamaal Lolesi
Keith Senior	4	4	Willie Tonga
Marcus Bai	5	5	Trent Cutler
Kevin Sinfield	13	6	Braith Anasta
Danny McGuire	6	7	Corey Hughes
Ryan Bailey	8	8	Chris Armit
Andrew Dunemann	14	9	Adam Perry
Danny Ward	15	10	Roy Asotasi
Jamie Jones-Buchanan	18	11	Reni Maitua
Chris McKenna	12	12	Sonny Bill Williams
Gareth Ellis	20	13	Tony Grimaldi
Willie Poching	16	15	Ben Czislowski
Barrie McDermott	10	17	Adam Brideson
Rob Burrow	7	16	Nate Myles
Ali Lauitiiti	11	14	Brett Oliver

Walker, Calderwood, McGuire Poching, Burrow, Mathers, Jones-Buchanan	Tries	El Masri 2, Patten Lolesi 2, Grimaldi
Sinfield 5	Goals	El Masri 4
Sinfield	Drop goals	

Referee: Sean Hampstead (Australia)

IN NOVEMBER 1969 Leeds had somewhat spuriously been crowned European Champions when beating their French counterparts Perpignan in a match conjured up by the BBC to test the advent of colour television. There was nothing phoney about the clash against Australia's best just over 35 years later as the Super League champions faced the NRL's leading side, Canterbury. There were many who thought that the Bulldogs had ready-made excuses if they were defeated, that they were not fully committed to the contest and underestimated its significance, but with their pride and reputation on the line they produced a second half fight back worthy of the event which worried the Rhinos to the core. Leeds fans, though, will forever wallow in the memories of a glorious first forty minutes, the equal of anything the side had served up in a big game to that point.

Yet it took skipper Kevin Sinfield's late, calming drop goal to finally serve up the spoils which marked a new chapter in blue and amber history. Here Danny McGuire recalls his decisive contribution to the Rhinos becoming the best side on the planet; scoring one of his most memorable touchdowns and having a hand or foot in four of their others. After a 32 year wait for a title, two trophies had come along almost at once.

OBVIOUSLY YOU QUALIFY TO play in such a prestigious match as the 2005 World Club Challenge by winning a Grand Final and I was lucky enough to have scored the decisive try at Old Trafford to clinch victory over the Bradford Bulls the previous October. That was a very special moment, the team at the time was being questioned as to whether it had the bottle to win the competition, even though we'd been the most dominant side during the regular season. We'd lost to Bradford in the play-offs and then been written off by many when we came up against them again on the big night. Plenty of people were saying that we couldn't handle the big games and I was the lucky one who got the headlines when we proved that we could. It was a terrific team effort and what made it even more memorable was that so many of the team were local mates who'd come through the Academy together and built a bond of genuine, close friendship; that was extra-special.

At the time of that touchdown to seal victory over the Bulls, the significance of it further down the line is farthest from your mind, all you can feel is euphoria, especially with so many team mates jumping on your back and celebrating. As things settled down a bit in the aftermath, the next focus was on the World Club Challenge and facing the best side in Australia. I'd played for Great Britain in the Tri-Nations following our success and lost to the Kangaroos, so the chance to play them again at club level couldn't come soon enough for me. If I'm honest now, I was disappointed to be on the bench for the international final having broken through during the tournament. At the time, because it was my first involvement at that level, I was just happy to be there and involved and around all the great players we had in the squad. A few weeks afterwards there was the feeling that I probably did deserve to start the game. The Aussies were red hot that night and gave us a good hiding and by the time I came on, in a way, I had nothing to lose which probably eased a lot of the pressure on me. In the long run, it might not have been a bad thing, I was able to just go out and enjoy the moment without it harming my development but it was a blow.

Throughout the 2004 campaign I'd been involved in a battle with Lesley Vainikolo to see who would finish as the top try scorer and although the press and fans built it up into something of a duel, to me it was never an issue. It's always nice for your ego to cross the whitewash but it's never been a priority for me. I've been more concerned with the team doing well, being successful and whoever took the individual honours and plaudits along the way would look after itself. I'll admit that I was disappointed when Les crossed for a few in the final game to just overtake me but I remember Tony Smith pulling me aside and saying, "don't worry, we'll come strong, look at the bigger picture," and that's exactly how it worked out in the end. The only score that mattered was the last one of the domestic season.

IN 2005, UNLIKE TWO YEARS later when we faced Melbourne in the same one-off World Club encounter, there was no lead in to the match. Against the Storm we had four Super League rounds to build up to the clash but when we opposed Canterbury that was our first proper game of the season. Tony was always a big believer in not looking too far ahead and taking each game as it came, to use the sporting cliché. He didn't want to talk up a match that was a couple of months away when we were in pre-season but just looked at each friendly as it arose. As a player, though, it was hard to get the World Club Challenge out of your mind and it was what we were training hard for. When we were struggling to run up the notorious Roundhay hills what kept us going was the thought of being world champions.

The World Club venue meant a lot to me on a couple of counts, not least because being a big Leeds United fan. Elland Road was somewhere that held a certain magic for me. That disastrous Tri-Nations final had been held there and I had the chance to put that horror show right within three months and wipe out the bad memory. I'd so looked forward to running out on the sacred turf and, on both occasions, the crowd was unbelievable. For the Rhinos, it was something else, virtually everyone in the sold out ground were blue and amber fans. I'd been to some fantastic nights there supporting United when it had been packed out, Champions League games included, but the atmosphere against Canterbury was even better than that. Rhinos fans are well known for being vocal and they made it sensational. When I was younger I played a bit of soccer although rugby and cricket were my main passions so I never thought I'd ever get the chance to play at such a prestigious place. To have the home dressing room and think that it was where some of my boyhood heroes had sat before doing battle was a tremendous feeling. It was great for my family as well because they were huge United fans so that lent something to the occasion for them also.

In some of the lead up to the game and analysis of it, there was mention that the referee was an Aussie who was unknown to us and he might favour Canterbury's style of play but it was never discussed among us as players. We were more concerned with what we were going to do and how we wanted to perform without letting outside influences become involved. We got the impression that the match meant a lot to the Canterbury squad who came over. Obviously there was much said and written about who didn't come and that they weren't a full strength side having left the likes of Willie Mason at home and how it didn't suit their fixtures which did annoy a lot of our boys. There was an impression given through the press that they were fulfilling the fixture because they had to but we never thought that was fair or the case. It did annoy us a little bit when people started talking like that but we were just trying to be professional and go out there and perform. The tag of being a potential World Champion was incentive and prestigious enough. Canterbury did have plenty of top liners in their ranks including current internationals like Sonny Bill Williams, Hazim El Mazri, Braith Anasta and Roy Asotasi and, if you look back, pretty much all of their side that played then have by now made 50 or so appearances in the NRL which proved their pedigree and no gloss can be taken off the final outcome and our performance, no matter what the Aussies may say.

We had Gareth Ellis on debut and he was an immediate influence in and around the dressing room. You could tell from day one that he was going to add a lot to the squad but he was the first to admit that he didn't feel as though he should collect a medal because he hadn't contributed to us attaining the right to play in that match. There has been a lot of talk, especially after 2007, about whether the World Club Challenge being played at the start of the next season when squads have changed as players retire, move on or come in, is the right time. That makes it a different squad to the ones that win the respective Grand Finals and I think that may alter if the seasons can be brought more in line and played so as to definitively end each campaign. In 2005 we'd lost Dave Furner, who'd been such a vital part of us winning Super League and it would have been a fitting tribute to him if he could have played in a World Club decider in his final match.

TONY SMITH WAS METICULOUS and in-depth in his game preparation, there was little he missed about the opposition and we did a lot of video work on Canterbury as individuals and the way they played as a team. We had the time to do that but they possibly didn't know as much about us, if I'm honest, and that probably worked to our advantage. He left no stone unturned and made sure that we knew exactly what we would be up against so there was no real need for too many last instructions from him or the coaching staff as we went out on the night.

We made a great start on the back of a couple of uncharacteristic errors from them. Gaz Ellis's break sent Chev inside Luke Patten, who then

misjudged Sinny's long kick for Calders to pounce. I think they were surprised with how well and strongly we began and the tempo we played at.
There were a few scuffles early on and that seemed to rile them. I don't
think that they expected us to be as physical as we were. To then show the
skill we did for first Chev and then Calders with his renowned pace to score
caught them a little off guard. We had to be good enough to capitalise on
their mistakes and we were.

What got them back in the game, almost single-handedly it seemed, was
Sonny Bill. He was sensational and set up their first try to revive them. I'd
played against him in the internationals at the end of 2004 and he'd got rid
of me a few times and slipped some fantastic off loads away. I remember
thinking at the time how incredibly strong he was but also what a massive
natural talent. That night for the Bulldogs, he was getting seemingly
impossible passes away for fun and then there was the ferocity of his
shoulder charges. One, in particular, on Marcus Bai stands out. Marcus was
one of the hardest guys around in his position and putting him on his back
just didn't happen. Sonny took the game on himself and got his side back
into contention, especially when El Masri added a touchline goal. That
didn't really affect us too much or put doubts in our minds, we were
always confident and believed we had the tools to win and win well. We
had a good, strong pack and a powerful threat out wide that could always
score tries but they came back well. Kev pulled us all in behind the posts
and told us to stick to the game plan and keep the pressure on and we did
that immediately.

Fortunately, I managed to score what ranks as one of the most memorable tries of my career. A lot of it was just instinct, I remember following
Barrie Mac and he got a superb off load away. Most of the time when
you're making half or full breaks, a natural impulse takes over but I did
momentarily recall doing something similar for Great Britain at Wigan in
the earlier Tri-Nations. Then, I'd passed an inside ball to Stu Reardon and
he got cleaned up and smashed. This was a similar sort of scenario, especially when as I was arcing away, Marcus Bai came in off his wing wanting
the ball from me. I got a momentary flashback to the Test match, dummied
and just backed myself to get to the corner. Looking back, I wish I'd also
done that for the international team but you learn from your mistakes and
that's what helped me squeeze in by the corner post. I could sense the fans'
anticipation when I broke clear around half way and the whole ground
rising during the run, although they weren't sure whether I'd touched
down in the field of play or been knocked into touch. Once the try was

given via the replay, the roar was unbelievable and the boys all started jumping on each other. It lifted us as a team and it's one of my best memories from the night, definitely.

It didn't erase the bad memories of what had happened on that ground in the Tri-Nations decider, I don't think those sorts of desperately disappointing thoughts ever go away. They do make you a better player, spur you on and drive you but they don't ever leave you or get replaced. They are something you should always hold in the back of your mind and store to make sure they never happen again. Because of them, you appreciate the good times – like that try – even more.

We had a superb finish to the first half, picking up two tries, which ultimately won us the game. Willie Poching, unusually, got the first, being in the right place to get on the end of another kick that bounced back and it was fantastic that such a servant as him, to the game as a whole as well as at Leeds, should get his name in the record books in such a way. We followed that with a spectacular team try that went through nine pairs of hands down our left hand side. Rob Burrow anticipated it really well pushing down the middle as he does so effectively and it was a fantastic effort with everyone supporting, backing each other up and not being afraid to move the ball about and chance their arm. That was how we played in 2004, we were the team with the most offloads and tended to convert our opportunities but none better than that score.

We went in 22-6 ahead, in as near a perfect position as we could have wished, but we knew the match wasn't yet won. Tony's team talks were always very relaxed, he only ever gave us a rollocking if we needed one, and basically he just told us to keep doing what we were and putting the pressure on, especially through our kicking game which seemed to be producing errors for us to capitalise on. We were talking among ourselves about trying to put 50 points on them and we were confident that we could. It was all really positive, the dressing room was buzzing and we couldn't wait to get back out there. They scored from around half-way straight after the re-start and although that might have altered our outlook a little bit, all the talk was about ensuring that it was the only try they were going to get. We just focused on the next set from the kick-off and restricting their yardage so that we could get back in control of the contest.

We achieved that by crossing twice in two minutes and both came from kicks as per the masterplan. I'd been doing some work with kicking guru Dave Alred in the lead up and it paid off. I got a decent one away for Richie and then Jonesy chased one down like a mad man, like he always does, and was there to capitalise on another mistake – surprisingly from Hazem El Masri – to pounce on the loose ball.

At 38-12 that should have been game over. The Bulldogs then hit a purple patch which brought them four tries in fifteen minutes to set up a much tenser finish than it should have been. They shouldn't have been anywhere near as close as six points, or one converted try. We'd been dominant and they got a roll on but it was early in the season for us, we'd only played a couple of friendlies and we were nowhere near as tuned up as we wanted to be. We were still working on a lot of things in training and, to their credit, they capitalised on that when they had a run of possession. There were a few nervy moments towards the end but I don't think that we ever felt in danger of letting it slip. It might not have appeared to the crowd that we were still in control but out on the pitch we still felt we were.

Kevin's drop goal close on time definitely sealed it. He's a great leader and, as he's done throughout his career, he knew the right time to pop one over to put us two scores ahead. We wanted to make the point of finishing the stronger. It was a terrific team effort and although it was nice, don't get me wrong, to be nominated as the man of the match, I'm not really one for individual accolades. Everyone loves to get the plaudits, I was just pleased for all the squad because we'd worked so hard in pre-season to achieve that goal and the season before to give us the opportunity to even be there. It was a real personal honour to get the award and when we picked up the trophy again, to see my name engraved on there, among some fantastic performers that have won it, was a tremendous thrill especially the thought that it will be there for posterity.

The noise of the fans as we went on the lap of honour was awesome. I remember looking up for my family but they were spread throughout all parts of the stadium. I managed to catch a glimpse of my girlfriend and Mum and Dad and those are the very best of times for me, with the realisation that you've actually done it and the high fiving among the lads and hugging each other. Those are the special memories, perhaps even more so than the game. You never forget them. Leeds United manager Kevin Blackwell was one of the first in the dressing room afterwards to join in the celebrations and congratulations. He'd been around us a bit and formed something of a partnership with Tony. We'd met their players a few times, which was great for me as a fan, and there was a bit of a link between the clubs at the time. It was nice of him – and some of his boys – to be in there and a part of it in his home stadium. It was terrific for the city as a whole.

We genuinely felt that we were the best team in the sport, although it's hard in a team sport to personally call yourself a world champion. It's different if you're, say, a sprinter and I don't think any of our guys were big noting it around town saying, "look at us, we're the best there is" or anything like that but it was great for the club to use it as a promotional tag and secure extra sponsorship on the back of it. It was nice for us every time we ran out during the domestic season to hear that we were being referred to by that title and that did boost the ego a bit but, more than that, was the pride that goes with being part of the side which achieved it. The shame was that the win over the Bulldogs represented our season's high point. We played well in the immediate aftermath but come the end of the campaign, when some key injuries struck, we'd lost a little of our spark and went down in the two domestic finals which was desperately disappointing.

IN 2008, THE EQUIVALENT World Club contest with Melbourne, also at Elland Road, was even more intense but the significance afterwards was just the same. I bitterly regret saying in an interview after we'd won the 2007 Grand Final that it felt better even than our success in 2004. That first time, I couldn't have got a better feeling from the victory and from scoring late on and when I think about my career, every such high point has been really special in its own right and you can't compare which means more. The success over the Storm was brutal, we were told afterwards that it was the first match on record that contained over 800 tackles and that Matt Diskin and Dallas Johnson had accounted for something like 60 each, which was phenomenal.

The matches against the Aussie champions couldn't have been more of a contrast, in 2005 it was free flowing and although the temperature was cold, conditions were conducive. You could play open rugby, that was what we were good at and Canterbury had a lot of flair players as well so that was why there was nearly a point a minute. Two years later, the wind and rain mixed in with the extreme cold was unbelievable, the worst you could think of for encouraging expansive play. We just had to grind it out, which was foreign to our normal game of throwing the ball about and producing something pleasing on the eye. But, from one to seventeen everyone in the side put their hand up and body on the line.

For me, that culminated in a shoulder injury and being led from the same side of the field at roughly the same time I was scoring my try three years earlier. It was incredibly frustrating and disappointing. As soon as I got taken out having kicked downfield I knew something was wrong straight away and tried to get out on to the wing to get my shoulder seen to. Obviously, they were a smart side, spotted that potential weakness immediately and attacked again down there. They ran at me and I had to make a tackle on Steve Turner as they pushed the ball wide before the physio could get on which didn't help. It's hard when you're being led off in such a close, fierce battle in the knowledge you won't be coming back on. You don't want to be too negative but I was all doom and gloom back in the changing rooms, it was like the world had ended. Once I got my head round the situation, I went back out to support the lads like you have to do and, when we emerged victorious, I tried to celebrate as best I could with my arm in a sling and not feel too sorry for myself. In our game, you get ups and downs like that and it was just unlucky for me that I had to come off. I know people might say that I didn't play a part in recapturing the trophy, but I was out there in the heart of it for 25 minutes and had a bit of a say in the outcome, contributed a little and I don't think anyone can take that away from me.

A COUPLE OF WEEKS AFTER the win over Canterbury, I signed a new five year deal with Leeds. There had been speculation that I might move to the NRL and presumably that win had again shown the Aussies some of the talent we had over here but, being a local lad and with the club so obviously going places, I had no desire to be anywhere else. When I was younger, I just played all sports purely because I enjoyed it so much. I could never have dreamt or expected to be a world champion, let alone one twice in three seasons. Coming from a real sporting family where my dad, uncles and grandad had all played, it was just a natural progression although I was the first one to take that tradition down rugby league lines. I'd wandered down to East Leeds as a six year-old and, as they do with all the new players, was put on the wing to keep me out the way. I might only have touched the ball three times that season but that didn't matter.

The next year, when I went out there again the coach just said, "no lad, get yourself in the middle" and I've played scrum half and then stand off for the rest of my life. That was the making of me and the honours that have followed in Leeds' recent rich history have been beyond my wildest dreams. I've been fortunate to come along during a great era for the club which hopefully will continue.

Representing the city of Leeds on a world stage has been very important to me, there is a genuine civic pride in everyone who comes from here and we support anyone who carries the name in whatever sport or walk of life.

When I was growing up, Leeds United was the big thing and their players were idolised and now the Rhinos are getting ever more popular and high profile thanks to what we are achieving. The club have a fantastic philosophy of promoting lads from the city through the Academy and putting immense time and effort into their development and improvement. I've been lucky to come through that fantastic coaching set up and been pointed in the right direction. I've always been immensely proud to come from Leeds.

ROB BURROW

SCRUM-HALF 2001–PRESENT

BORN   26 September 1982
SIGNED   From Featherstone Juniors and made his way through the Academy ranks
LEEDS CAREER (to end of 2007)   209 appearances, 99 tries, 120 goals, 2 drop goals
HONOURS   Grand Final 2004, 2007, runner-up 2005; World Club Challenge 2005; Challenge Cup runner-up 2003, 2005; 5 Great Britain caps, 10 England caps, 2 Yorkshire appearances

2007 was Rob Burrow's year, the 'pocket rocket' garnering a host of prestigious individual awards after a momentous season of consistently electrifying performances. 'Player of the Year' at the Rhinos in their title winning campaign, announced as man of the match in the Grand Final, and, finally, nominated as Player of the Series for Great Britain as they whitewashed the Kiwis. Blistering pace off the mark, a wonderful side step, instinctive support play and a brave cover tackler, he is ostensibly the best pound-for-pound exponent around. The scorer of some memorable tries, none more so than his wonderful effort in the 2005 World Club Challenge against Canterbury, Burrow ended the 2007 campaign on the verge of a century of touchdowns for the club, while his percentage success ratio with the boot ranks him alongside the very best.

Leeds Rhinos 33 v St Helens 6

Super League Grand final
Saturday 13 October 2007

Old Trafford
Attendance 71,352

*Leeds dismantle St Helens with arguably the finest display
in the club's history*

Teams

Brent Webb	1	1	Paul Wellens
Lee Smith	5	2	Ade Gardner
Clinton Toopi	3	3	Matt Gidley
Keith Senior	4	4	Willie Talau
Scott Donald	2	5	Francis Meli
Danny McGuire	6	6	Leon Pryce
Rob Burrow	7	7	Sean Long
Kylie Leuluai	8	8	Nick Fozzard
Matt Diskin	9	9	Keiron Cunningham (captain)
Jamie Peacock	10	10	Jason Cayless
Jamie Jones-Buchanan	11	11	Lee Gilmour
Gareth Ellis	12	30	Chris Flannery
Kevin Sinfield (captain)	13	12	Jon Wilkin
Ryan Bailey	16	14	James Roby
Ian Kirke	18	15	Mike Bennett
Carl Ablett	22	17	James Graham
Ali Lauitiiti	14	22	Maurie Fa'asavalu
Webb, Lauitiiti, Donald, Smith, Jones-Buchanan	Tries		Roby
Sinfield 6	Goals		Long
Burrow	Drop goals		

Referee: Ashley Klein

DEBATE AMONG RHINOS FANS in the giddy aftermath of securing their second title in four seasons was whether the eighty minute display their favourites had served up was the finest team performance in the club's illustrious history. The way Leeds dismantled an outstanding St Helens side – who were the defending champions – brought comparisons with the 1923, 1936 and 1978 Challenge Cup final teams and those which had secured the 1961 Championship and 1979 Premiership for the Loiners. On balance, the 2007 vintage can justifiably lay claim to producing the best all-round display of them all, not least because of the undeniable quality of their opponents. Outstanding defensively in the first half to douse the Saints' fire, Tony Smith's men exhibited exceptional flair after the interval to bring the Super League trophy back to Headingley Carnegie, inculcating a glorious style and panache for which the blue and amber is renowned.

At the heart of it was swashbuckling scrum half Rob Burrow, who here recounts his memories of a magnificent contribution.

Six weeks before the play-offs started, having suffered three defeats in their previous four games, some of the natives were becoming restless, but the Rhinos squad produced an irresistible run of simply sensational form to take them to ultimate glory. Having won two Grand Finals and made a third, been World Club Champions for the first time and appeared in two Challenge Cup finals, from the start of 2003 to that exceptional evening at Old Trafford, there is little doubt that the current crop are serving up the club's third golden age and is on course to become part of Leeds rugby league's greatest ever era.

EVERYTHING CAME GOOD IN the final weeks of Super League XII for Leeds Rhinos. We finally changed the perception that we are 'bottlers' and underachievers; the 'nearly men' tag has well and truly gone. To win the title twice in four years is some achievement, along with all the other trophies and finals but, importantly, we've been involved every year right to the end. That sort of consistency is the sign of a great side. In the past, there has been a huge weight of expectation, understandably so with a club this size, and it is fantastic being part of sides that are now, regularly, achieving their potential.

When we lost to Saints at Knowsley Road in the 2007 play-offs, in one of the toughest domestic matches ever, we knew that we had more to give and could kick on whereas we felt they had peaked and that if we did meet them in the Grand Final we could win the ultimate prize. Wigan stood in our way, back at Headingley Carnegie but we were on a roll, nobody was going to stop us and we delivered. Sometimes there are teams you cannot pin down. That season it was the Warriors. They did something right as they got three out of three wins during the regular season over us. In the play-offs, we owed them one and there was extra incentive to beat them and beat them well. If we won by just two points, we'd be at Old Trafford, fantastic, but the way we went about it that night gave us an extra buzz in the changing room. We hammered them and I've never known anything like the confidence we felt afterwards as we celebrated victory – but it could have been any team we faced that night, we would have beaten them. We were on fire.

GROWING UP NEAR CASTLEFORD, which is such a massive rugby league town, you could not help but follow the sport. Dad is from Leeds and took me to games at Headingley, so I always supported the club. My first match was Leeds versus Leigh. I was six and got mixed up because the names of the teams were so similar. We sat at the back of the stand and although I didn't know what was really going on, it was exciting. I liked watching the British stars, like Wigan and Leeds legend Ellery Hanley, but my hero quickly became Brisbane, Queensland and Australia scrum half Alfie Langer. When you see guys like him performing so magnificently at the highest level, it inspires you to believe that you too can make it. Langer was always ripping Great Britain apart and, being small, I clicked onto him.

I joined Featherstone Juniors and loved it. They have a great youth set up and because it is renowned as an area for breeding talent, scouts came to watch the big games and the youth team finished as Yorkshire champions.

I heard Leeds talent spotter Bob Pickles, who is responsible for so many of the great youngsters signing up to the club since the Academy system was introduced, was coming over to watch me and that did make me a little nervous. After he'd seen me play a few times, I was invited to a couple of weekend camps during the summer holidays. I felt under pressure and was desperate to perform because the chance meant everything to me. I signed after the first camp, it was a dream come true for a 13-year-old kid but there were no guarantees. I've been tied to Leeds ever since.

Having joined the academy, the senior team got to the Challenge Cup final in 1999 and we were taken along to Wembley to support them. We sat in the corner where most of Leeds' second half tries were scored, it was a great vantage point and inspiring. Feeling even a small part of the club as it won the trophy was special.

Dean Bell was in charge of the youngsters at Headingley and it was a strict environment. He was a legend in the game, big on discipline and got the best out of us. I played in three sides at different ages. Many lads moved on but ten of us were in the squad that won the 2004 Grand Final against Bradford, which was amazing. I was a substitute that night at Old Trafford and delighted to be part of the side which won the first trophy since that Cup win, but having a bigger role in 2007 made that triumph especially memorable. Six of us who came through together played in both matches. The system and structure is so good that it will continue to develop talent.

Our goals every year are to win everything we enter and, with the talent and back up available to us, that's an achievable aim rather than an arrogant boast. It was a huge disappointment in 2007 to go out of the Challenge Cup early doors at home to Wigan but it proved to be a blessing in disguise because there were then blank weeks in the Super League programme when we could recover from knocks. There are so many tough games nowadays, although the intimidating grounds are no longer there in the same way. I was only a teenager when I first played at the Boulevard against Hull, for example. Fans were rocking the cage as we came out and it was daunting but I now enjoy performing at the KC Stadium. Coming from Cas, I'm often on the receiving end from home supporters at the Jungle but it's a great ground as the fans are close to the action.

As the season develops, the intensity of training increases as the prizes come into view. Individually and collectively you prepare the same but mentally you know that what you have been working hard for all year is within touching distance. Routines tend not to vary and for a home game I'm usually one of the first at Headingley. I like to get a massage to warm my legs up, have a laugh with the lads who arrive early and stay relaxed. Some boys concentrate quietly and everyone builds up in a different way. There are plenty of mickey takers especially Scott Donald, Jamie Peacock and myself. I keep the serious thinking until ten minutes before we go out to warm up. Most of the pre-match discussion has taken place so it's a question of trigger points. The lads know what needs to be done.

Most teams go off in ones and twos at half-time and at full time but we've always been a close bunch so jog on and off together through good and bad. Inevitably new players come in but the spirit remains the same. It can be hard for a nervous youngster coming into such an environment. When I started, Barrie McDermott came over and immediately introduced himself. I'll never forget that and we're still good mates. When new players sign or young lads come in I always make a point to help them settle.

THE DEBATE ABOUT WHETHER it's better to go straight to the Grand Final or play an extra qualifying game happens every season. We have finished top of Super League and won the Grand Final, finished top and lost one and now finished second and taken the prize, so I guess that proves there is no answer. In 2007, we'd have liked to have taken the most direct route but without the Wigan win we may not have performed as we did in Manchester. We were disappointed after the St Helens play-off defeat in the qualifying match. We didn't play as we could have but only lost by a penalty goal. We had an ideal chance to put that right the following week and playing gets you battle-hardened. You're on a roll; less juice but fired up. Rest or play can work both ways but, in the end, the best team always wins.

The other great debate is where the Grand Final stacks up against the Challenge Cup. Everyone around the world who follows rugby league is aware of the Cup. I remember watching Wigan hammer everybody at Wembley when I was a kid, so to be a part of its history and be involved at a packed Wembley would be amazing. The final has moved around in recent years but when you think of the Challenge Cup, as a player, you think of Wembley and it's great that the final is back there again. I'd give anything to go there and win but like many modern day players my opinion of where it stands compared to the Grand Final has changed. If I had to choose to win just one, it would be the championship decider because it is the culmination of a season's achievement, with the best two teams battling it out.

Any side can enjoy a good draw, hit a bit of form at the right time and reach the Cup final.

Mentally the last few weeks of a Super League season are massive. Every team knows that finishing in the top two is an advantage – it buys you a life – and gives you a home run. Taking the League Leader's Shield is a mark of consistency but, more importantly, you need a different attitude to handle the play-offs. You must step up, although you can't put your finger on it and just when you think that matches can't get quicker or tougher, they do. Fitness levels and expectations are higher every season, so you have to keep raising the bar.

All the top sides have won and lost major finals since the Super League era began. In 2005, we did not quite have it in both the Challenge Cup and the Grand Final after a terrific regular season. Losing them was tough but we learnt so much in defeat and that came into our preparations for 2007's visit to Old Trafford. We discussed what drives you to win and the disappointment of losing finals. You have to take something from defeat and we did. We wanted to feel as we did in 2004 when we won the Grand Final and that was a massive motivator. The bitter 2005 experience will continue to help us in future years.

OUR PREPARATION FOR THE 2007 Grand Final followed our normal training routine and then the night before the Saints game we sat in a circle and described what winning meant to each of us. For me this was a big part of our preparation. It was something I'll never forget and I understood what the ultimate success truly meant to everyone in the squad. I shared a room with Danny McGuire, probably because they wanted to keep those in similar positions together. It never bothers me who I room with because they are all great lads and that 2007 squad was something special.

Brent Webb was new to the side that year but we knew we were getting a world-class full-back and he didn't disappoint. Throughout the season, he scored and set up fantastic tries and made a huge, unselfish contribution. Although a stand out individual, he always did what was best for the team. Scott Donald had an absolutely fantastic year, his raw pace frightened defences and he got on the end of a lot of our expansive play. Knowing you have an out and out finisher does wonders for the confidence of those inside him to create chances because the likelihood is that if you get him any kind of space, he will score. That was only one side of his game, though. His covering back was superb and he was always willing to run the ball in where it hurt. Lee Smith over the last couple of years has been the best young player at Leeds and will probably go on to play for Great Britain. He is so versatile, originally a full-back, he can play at half-back or even dummy half if necessary. To have someone with such a utility value is a huge asset in the modern game.

Centres Clinton Toopi and Keith Senior are big, strong men. Toops can smash opponents, it's a big part of his game. I've been at the side of him on tackles and he absolutely rocks them back. Keith has been there and done it for club and country for over a decade. Massive when running out wide, he is like a back up second rower on defence and never shirks. As for Danny McGuire, we know each other inside out and continue to grow as a partnership each year. He has world-class skills on attack but throughout 2007 became much more of an all round player for the team. He worked incredibly hard on his defence and as a play maker. Having Brent in the side gives so many options on supporting a break, Danny can now create tries rather than having to be on the end of them all and that makes him even more dangerous. He is also deceptively quick.

Our pack was simply awesome. Kylie Leuluai is one of the hardest hitters I've seen and St Helens knew all about that from the play-off game when he absolutely smashed them. He came with the reputation of being a strongman, which embarrasses him a little, but it was immediately obvious as soon as we saw him in the gym that it was true. He was massive for us as the season wore on and has that bit of nastiness about him that is the hallmark of all the best front rowers. Opponents respect him and they know exactly what to expect.

I've never known anyone as passionate or proud for club and national team than Jamie Peacock. He gives his all in every game and his form in the final few weeks, when it really mattered, was simply awe-inspiring. Playing for Leeds means everything to him and he wore that on his sleeve which was immense for all of us.

Matt Diskin is a good old-fashioned hooker and is the perfect example of 'you don't know what you've got until it's gone'. Take him out of the side and you realise what a magnificent job he does. Disko is tough week in, week out, controls the vital ruck area and is a phenomenal defender with a tremendous work rate. Jamie Jones-Buchanan is another who is so proud to play for his home town club and has an absolutely enormous will to win. He showed great courage to overcome injuries that would have caused lesser men to retire early in their career and Tony Smith brought the best out of him. His form was so good that he won a Great Britain cap on the back of how he played in 2007, which was a fantastic, deserved achievement. Gareth Ellis is a top class back rower and respected around the world. Like Kylie, the way he hits is unbelievable and the best is still to come from him.

All the lads massively respect Kevin Sinfield. I have never met a more professional person and it shows on the pitch. He has every skill in the book, can play as a back or forward, is a world-class goal kicker and a natural leader. Kevin's consistency with the boot is amazing. You can see opponents sink a bit with every success, especially the tough ones, but we get used to it, we genuinely think he won't miss. To score from the corner and make it six points instead of four is massive because so many Super League games are tight.

On the bench, we had terrific options. Ali Lauitiiti is a big man and, when fit, other teams know it. In the last few games of the season, Ali showed why he's up there with the best in the world. He can do things with the ball other players barely dream of, he's unbelievable. Ryan Bailey is another who does the real grinding stuff and is respected by opponents because of it. When he comes off the bench, it gives us a lift and them something to think about. He is extremely intimidating. Ian Kirke is the quietest lad you could meet but big and powerful. When someone of his size and physical presence runs at you it takes a lot of energy to pull them down. He has worked incredibly hard to improve and deserved his chance. It's the same with Carl Ablett, another whose dream it was to play for Leeds. He overcame the trauma of having to miss almost a year through a knee reconstruction but stayed strong mentally and took his opportunity when it finally came. Being involved in a Grand Final can only boost his confidence further. Like them, I was on the bench in 2004 and being involved in and part of a match of such stature makes you desperate to kick on.

It was the same going through the Saints ranks, we respected them and their abilities especially as we knew so many of them from playing together internationally. Paul Wellens is consistently the best British full-back around, Ade Gardner a proven finisher of the highest quality and Matt Gidley has done everything at the top level. He is a wonderful player with great hands. Willie Talau combines strength and speed, he has it all and Francis Meli, outside him, is so difficult to put down, they make a great pairing.

Leon Pryce was the one player above all we named as a real danger. He is such a threat with ball in hand because of his unpredictability. You can't afford to take your guard down for a second with him or he'll be away. We expected Sean Long to play even though he was an injury doubt in the lead up. His influence is massive, especially his kicking game and we knew Saints would do all they could to have him out there directing operations.

Up front, we expected a typically ferocious battle to match the intensity of the play-off game. Nick Fozzard had had a great season, often taking the first carry and putting his hand up for the hard yards. Likewise Jason Cayless, whose best work often goes unnoticed. Keiron Cunningham has caused Leeds – and virtually every other club – damage over the years. A master of his craft, we knew that our defensive pride in our line had to at least match his desire to get over it from close in, which was his trademark. Lee Gilmour is another very fine player who frequently finds his best game against Leeds. Chris Flannery was relatively new in for Saints but came with a great reputation and was starting do an excellent job, while I have known and admired Jon Wilkin since Academy days.

On the bench, St Helens weren't short of talent either boasting, like us, some of the best emerging British stars around, which made the contest even more exciting and anticipated. James Graham has a huge future ahead of him and looks set to be at the top for a long time and the same is true of James Roby who won the Man of Steel award in 2007, somewhat controversially but rightfully so. He has the ability to influence a game at key moments and is such a danger to tiring markers out of dummy half when he comes on. Tackling Maurie Fa'asavalu knocks a lot out of you and Mike Bennett always does a solid job.

BECAUSE OF LIKELY MOTORWAY traffic and the occasion, we arrived at Old Trafford two hours before kick-off. Looking around our changing room all the guys were focused. We'd said all that needed to be in the emotional lead up and now it was down to action and we couldn't wait. Walking out for a major final is always special, you are in awe of the event but you soon settle down. Old Trafford is such a great ground and so far, for me, it's the ultimate. Nerves don't come into it, if you feel them then you have to turn it into energy. The day before, anticipation is great and you can't wait to see a full stadium. Then suddenly you are out there and it's better than you imagined. You just want to get on with the game and we needed a big start.

Both teams were up for it and Saints should have taken an early lead when Disko blocked Sean Long 20 metres out but he pushed his penalty attempt wide. Psychologically we had won the first minor skirmish. They could reasonably have been expected to be in front but they weren't and we grew even more confidence from that. Saints had us on the back foot and we had to be strong to stop Jon Wilkin on the last tackle but soon had our own period of pressure. Nick Fozzard stripped the ball from Gareth Ellis and Kevin edged us into the lead with his boot, so it was a double whammy, we'd taken our first chance for points whereas they hadn't. That successful kick meant Kevin became the first Leeds player to play and score in every game in a season, which was a fantastic effort and another deserving place for him in the club's record books.

It had been important to keep Saints out but we gained even greater resolve from our first try, which was a brilliant sweeping effort that showed what we were best at, quick off loads and close support play. Brent Webb is the finishing master and he got over in the corner after some fantastic work by Danny and Kev. When moves like that come off, everyone feels a real boost and when Kevin kicked the conversion from the touchline, we had the sort of fantastic start we were looking for.

We were doing well in general play but there were spells when Saints got going, although I still felt we were dominating. They are renowned fighters and proved it with James Roby doing what he does best when he entered the battle. Sean Long started a great move that caught us up the middle and James finished superbly despite Lee Smith's best efforts. They were back in the game. It was a great try but we made them work for it. I knew that things would come good for us because of the number of Leeds players that chased back. You could tell we really wanted it and were unlucky not to extend our lead when Danny brilliantly chipped over the Saints defence, gathered and kicked again to the corner for Scott to chase, but the ball just beat him to touch short of a brilliant score.

Just on half-time we had to dig deep to keep Saints out. I'm not sure they got the credit for how well they played in the first half – it was a terrific contest at tremendous pace – but we finished on the attack. We jogged off together as usual and looking at the guys I knew that if we raised the bar a little it would be our night. That was the theme of our chat in the changing room. We realised Saints would make a big push at the start of the second half so had to be ready for the challenge but came out determined to go up a couple of gears.

As expected, they put us under the gun a bit at the beginning of the second period and Sean Long kept us in our half with his clever kicking game. That was a crucial period of the game and we had to stay strong. We forced an error from Saints in their own half and Lee Smith came infield to set Ali free, who powered passed Matt Gidley to score an absolutely brilliant touchdown. It came at the perfect time and was such a big play. I don't know how many other players could have scored it. Ali had around

25 metres to run with the ball and to beat someone like Matt, a world class centre, on the outside, was fantastic. Every try is exciting but we all got in to celebrate that one because we could sense it was such a big moment.

Ali's try began an irresistible momentum. On the next set Webby and Keith combined on the blind side to set Scott away and he came up with one of the greatest scores seen in a Grand Final. Not many beat Paul Wellens on the outside but part of that was down to Brent continuing his run. For a second Paul was caught in two minds and against someone as quick as Scott, that was it, gone. To get back to back tries was fantastic. We were buoyant but none of us thought that we'd won it at that moment. I knew our confidence would continue to soar, we'd gone up a level but had to continue at the same intensity. The two scores were massive and took a lot out of Saints but a chance soon came my way to drop my first goal of the season. I slotted over and gave us a 13-point lead.

A three score advantage combined with the way we were playing seemed to drain Saints, especially as our defence stayed strong. Ten minutes from time, when Danny put up a pinpoint kick for Lee to time his leap perfectly and take before crossing, the game was up. As he touched down the excitement turned to realisation that we'd got 'em. Saints could have got on a roll with three quick tries, it's possible, but I didn't think they could do it on that night. Lee's effort was the game breaker. Kevin kicked the extras and soon added another penalty.

In the last minute, Jamie Jones-Buchanan powered over from close range to score our final try and with the very last kick of the game, Kevin made it 33-6. I knew we'd won before the end but, when the hooter goes, what you've achieved starts to sink in. We could finally stop running about battering each other. It was time to celebrate. It's impossible to describe that feeling of excitement, you have to savour the moment. I'll never forget the celebrations on the field and the presentation. It made all the hard work worthwhile.

Having being awarded the Man of the Match trophy, I was whisked off to the press conference, so missed 20 minutes in the dressing room. When I got back, there was total pandemonium, excitement, emotion and it really gets to you. You have no control over yourself. Everyone was thrilled because it meant so much to us all. It takes time to fully sink in and the following day I still couldn't quite believe that we'd done it.

SOME JOURNALISTS SAID OUR win was one of the greatest displays not only in Grand Final history but also for Leeds as a club. It was also seen as a fitting tribute to legend Jeff Stevenson who had died that morning. The fact that just over fifty years after he had won the Lance Todd trophy at Wembley, I was wearing the same shirt number and taking the Harry Sunderland Award was not lost on me, it only heightened the feeling of how special the whole night was.

From a personal viewpoint, that victory against St Helens was the finest performance I've been involved in with Leeds and it will take some beating. To find your best display of the season in the Grand Final is what it's all about. I was chuffed to bits with the Man of the Match award but you have to look at the team effort in general. The accolade was fantastic but the way our forwards were dominant was something else. They smashed Saints to bits and to be behind them was fantastic. The whole team played a massive part and there was no one individual that stood out.

It's a cliché but my career so far has been a dream come true. Winning domestic honours is amazing but the pinnacle for me was pulling on an international jersey. I led the England Academy side to New Zealand and Australia in 2001 and scored tries against France and Ireland in European Nations Cup wins in 2003 and 2004. A year later, I got my first call up to the Great Britain squad, went down under on tour and ended 2007 as the player of the series in the Tests against the Kiwis. I am immensely proud of all those performances.

Tony Smith brought the best out of every player at Leeds and changed the ethos at the club. He instilled in us a winning mentality. That in its own right is a massive feat. He developed my game, every skill has improved and to be voted Leeds Player of the Year by him in a season that we took the ultimate prize was another astonishing moment that I will never forget. It would have been a shame to have lost out in the Grand Final. For Tony to depart on a loss would not have reflected what he has done for Leeds Rhinos. Now supporters will remember him, like the players do, as an absolute winner. With him now in charge of the national team, I'm sure he'll get similar results. I'd love to be part of a winning Ashes and World Cup team. But none of that can happen without continuing to develop at Leeds.

It's been a privilege and a dream to play for Leeds, and to be a part of two Grand Final winning sides. It may not be until I finish playing that I really appreciate what it means but I do know how fortunate I am to play for a top club chasing honours every season.

Someone once told me that if you love your job then you'll never do a day's work in your life. That's what it's like playing for the Rhinos and I cannot wait to repeat our successes. Once you have tasted it, you want it again and there is always a new goal. In 2008, we set out to become the first Leeds team to retain the championship trophy and taste Wembley.